INTERIOR DESIGN WORKBOOK

PROBLEMS AND PROJECTS FOR 1ST AND 2ND YEAR STUDENTS

Nancy Temple

VNR VAN NOSTRAND REINHOLD
_____ New York

Copyright © 1993 by Van Nostrand Reinhold

Library of Congress Catalog Card Number 92-7476
ISBN 0-442-00953-4

Printed in the United States of America.

Van Nostrand Reinhold
115 Fifth Avenue
New York, New York 10003

Chapman and Hall
2-6 Boundary Row
London, SE1 8HN, England

Thomas Nelson Australia
102 Dodds Street
South Melbourne 3205
Victoria, Australia

Nelson Canada
1120 Birchmount Road
Scarborough, Ontario MIK 5G4, Canada

16 15 14 13 12 11 10 9 8 7 6 5 4 3 2 1

Library of Congress Cataloging-in-Publication Data

Temple, Nancy.
    Interior design workbook : problems and projects for 1st and 2nd year students / Nancy Temple.
        p.   cm.
    Includes index.
    ISBN 0-442-00953-4
    1. Interior decoration—Study and teaching (Higher)—United States.   I. Title.
NK2116.5.T46   1992
729—dc20
                                                                                            92-7476
                                                                                            CIP

CONTENTS

Section IV Space-Planning

Section V Selection of Furniture and Finish Materials

Section VI Human Factors

Section VII More Design Challenges

PREFACE

Interior design has evolved into a profession with ever greater concerns and responsibilities within the past two decades. The field includes not only generalists but many specialists who practice under the interior design umbrella, such as decorators, exhibit and set designers, space-planners, lighting designers, furniture and product designers, and so on. At the same time, many states have instituted licensing requirements for interior designers, and other states are sure to follow suit.

Partly in response to the increasing complexity and visibility of the field, more schools are granting certificates and degrees in interior design. The new programs are established in such diverse departments as art, graphic design, fashion design, and home economics. The backgrounds and interests of department chairpersons and instructors—many of whom are part-time teachers with design businesses that command much of their attention—naturally vary. Curricula also vary greatly. Some focus on the decoration of residential interiors, others on developing a facility in space-planning for systems furniture, whereas still others

emphasize an architectural approach.

As a student and, later, a teacher of interior design, I observed that the textbooks students were asked to purchase were books that emphasized the definition, history, and theory of design. Though often excellent, they were lengthy, and the amount of design work required of students precluded asking them to do much reading in these texts. Other books bought by students tended to be either general or specific reference books—again, excellent and necessary books in any designer's library. However, instructors had to invent or borrow the projects that they were assigning to students, perhaps with little guidance or assistance from chairpersons or colleagues. One result was that the quality of the projects was variable and that there was little consistency from one class to another. In addition, instructors teaching subjects in which they had little expertise found it difficult to locate programs and plans to use in projects. I encountered this problem many times in my own teaching career.

The freshman students I faced often had little or no knowledge of design or drafting. Their needs I saw as intellectual (the need to be stimulated, to create, to problem solve, to explore options), technical (the need to learn about both the possibilities and the restrictions within the field; the need, also, to learn the techniques and conventions of graphic expression), and, not least, psychological (the need to feel encouraged and excited about interior design). I felt that a workbook that could meet those needs would be of immense value. As such a book did not exist, I decided to write it, and thus *Interior Design Workbook* was born.

My goal has been to ensure that students using this book will learn a lot about the field and will enjoy the process. The projects within touch on the fundamental issues that concern designers, including the manipulation of space, programming, space-planning, the selection of furniture and finishes, human factors, and more. The book is intended to familiarize students with a wide variety of realistic design projects, to give them an understanding of the scope of the field, and to help them develop

the problem-solving skills and aesthetic judgement they will need to succeed in the world of interior design. In addition, I have tried throughout to make the text engaging and lively.

I am deeply indebted to my husband, Matthew Temple, and my parents, Simon and Annette Rottenberg, for helping me find the time to write the book. I also want to thank Jan Morse, who drafted many of the book's plans and elevations, in spite of her own busy schedule.

TO THE INSTRUCTOR

The purpose of this workbook is to provide you and your students with a wide variety of projects and exercises—small and large, residential and commercial. The projects vary in difficulty, and the range presented is suitable for students in both the first and second years of an interior design program.

The book is designed to be used with the greatest possible flexibility. It is expected that an instructor might realistically give between three and five assignments per semester. The large number of projects included here makes it possible for you to select exactly those problems that will benefit your particular class and to use the book for several semesters. For all projects, presentation requirements are indicated, but you can adjust these requirements to suit your class.

The projects are organized into eight major categories. In each group, there are problems of different sizes; some may be treated as one-day or one-week sketch problems, whereas others will require much more time.

Section I projects are intended for students who have not had art or design courses or who need review in such subjects. In addition, these projects can be completed even if students have not yet had instruction in architectural drafting, as the requirements are freehand sketches and models. The intent in including these projects is to provide very basic exercises. Some instructors may prefer not to use these projects at all, or they may want to have students complete them quickly—within the first two weeks of a semester, for example. These projects can also help instructors determine the level of competence of freshmen students. Perspective outlines provided both in this and other sections of the book may, if desired, be taken by the students to a reprographic service to be enlarged.

It is important to note that the problems throughout need not be assigned in the order in which they appear; for instance, some teachers may wish to begin with the Group Three exercises in programming. The workbook also contains some introductory and reference material to guide students in completing projects. It is not, however, intended to be in any way a substitute for lectures, visual aids such as slides, classes in drafting or presentation techniques, design textbooks that emphasize history or theory, or for comprehensive reference books.

TO THE STUDENT

If you are new to the study of interior design, you may wonder how the beautiful interior spaces that you admire both in life and in magazines came to be designed. How were they conceived? How do designers make choices? Where do they get their inspiration?

Actually, there are many answers to those questions. Much of what makes a designer good can be learned and is a matter of technique; there are formulas and tricks of the trade. The very best designers, however, are creative artists as much as painters or sculptors. They are the people who come up with new and unexpected solutions that surprise and delight everyone. Often, their innovations become standard practice for other designers who admire their work. There are also many designers who are better at some aspects of design than others and who, therefore, specialize within the field. Some examples are space-planners, lighting consultants, acoustical consultants, decorators, and renderers.

For a design solution to be successful, both functional and aesthetic requirements must be met. This means that although designers are concerned with the appearance of spaces, they also must be sure that user needs are fulfilled. It is not an exaggeration to say that, no matter how beautiful an interior is, its designer has failed if the space functions poorly or if its user is not comfortable (which is sometimes the same thing).

Some of the functional issues that arise in interior design projects include: space-planning—with attention to adequate clearances, adjacencies, and circulation space—user comfort, appropriate color choices, correct lighting, acoustics, planning for the handicapped, and concern with durability and maintenance of materials and furniture.

Aesthetic issues would include: developing a theme, image, or atmosphere through appropriate selections of colors, patterns, materials, and either built-in or moveable equipment or furniture. There are many other considerations, too, such as unity, contrast, symmetry, rhythm, and scale, which are pertinent to interior as well as graphic or product design.

To make sure that both the func-tional and aesthetic needs of the client are addressed, the designer must learn to think about all aspects of the problem simultaneously and automatically. This means that, while determining the configuration of interior walls, he is also thinking about how to furnish the space; while planning a kitchen, the lighting and selection of finishes are also being considered. The reason that these issues are not dealt with in a linear, or sequential, fashion is that each aspect of the design ultimately has an impact on other aspects. Therefore, changes made to the interior may affect decisions made about the location of windows, or the height of the ceiling. On the other hand, the decision to put large windows on an exterior wall to capture a beautiful view will help to determine the use to which the adjacent interior space is put; this space might be more likely to be "public" space, such as a living room, than "private" space, such as a bathroom. This same decision to introduce a large expanse of glass will affect the interior lighting plan.

Similarly, it is important to understand that the very act of sketching and drawing ideas gives the designer food for thought. In drawing a plan, problems of various kinds can be identified and corrected. The drawing inspires a response in its creator and by itself can be the impetus for further changes.

Thinking like a designer means knowing that every design decision is a deliberate one and must make sense. A client's trust would be severely undermined if her designer presented a plan with the words, "I don't know why I did it this way. I just like it." Nevertheless, students sometimes make the same statement during class presentations about their projects. Some design decisions may seem intuitive—may seem to appear from some unconscious area of the creative mind. If they are good decisions, however, they will be responsive to either the functional or the aesthetic demands of the project. Imagine a situation, for example, in which a designer is planning a kitchen. Decisions to solve problems relating to function might include installing a second sink or selecting a durable countertop material such as granite. On the other hand, let us say that the rectangular kitchen area is open to a breakfast nook with a curved wall of windows overlooking the garden. The designer may decide to install a curved or even circular island between kitchen and breakfast nook. Although the curve of the island does not contribute to its usefulness, the shape creates a relationship between the two spaces. Thus, the designer has found a way to make the entire space more interesting and more beautiful. Keep in mind that, whether you are presenting a project to a teacher or a client, your goals and decisions should be clear to you, and you should be able to explain and defend them. In the example just given, the designer would be able to state that the circular island was both inspired by and echoes the curve of the window wall and was not just a random or arbitrary shape.

Professional designers get their ideas from many sources. A store designer was once inspired by the black-and-white marble tiles she saw while travelling in India; a similiar pattern became the start of a complete and complicated interior renovation for a large New York department store. Another designer, working on the renovation of a penthouse apartment in New York, sat in the space and tried to visualize its interior layout. He gradually came to realize that the space reminded him of an Italian villa, except that the windows were too small. This associa-tion led him to the decision to make all the small, existing windows into doors that led out onto the terrace. Yet another designer, working on a showroom for office furniture, was intrigued by an exhibit of fluorescent light tubes that he had recently seen; the artist's method for mounting his light tubes was borrowed by the designer for his own project. Thus, we see that inspiration may come from an interest in using a specific material or color, and from recollections of things that we have seen, or places that we have been. It may derive from an attempt to suggest a historical style, from the desire to create a kind of stage set (especially in retail and restaurant interiors), from the need to highlight a particular piece of furniture or artwork—in short, ideas come from almost anyplace!

Lastly, understand that experience is a great teacher. The process of thinking about many aspects of the design project simultaneously becomes easier; your knowledge of available materials continually increases; ideas that have worked successfully in the past will make future projects better; the experiences you will share with other professionals will also become part of your ongoing education. This is only the beginning.

Section I
First Exercises in Basic Principles of Design

PROJECTS

1. **Recipe for a Kitchen: The Effects of Line, Repetition, and Rhythm in Design**

2. **Everything Old is New Again: Unity and Contrast**

3. **Bedroom Shades: Changes in Color and Pattern**

4. **Symmetry and Balance: A Living Room**

5. **Changes in Scale (and Size and Proportion): A Music Room**

The following projects introduce you to the most fundamental principles of design as they apply to the practice of interior design. They are intended to be completed fairly quickly, either as sketch problems in class or as homework. As each exercise is finished, it will be useful for the whole class to assemble, pin up sketches, and discuss the work. If, during these discussions, there is disagreement among members of your class concerning the results of the work, so much the better! In this early stage of design education, there should be lots of looking, thinking, and debating!

It should be noted that these principles of design are not limited to interior design but are considerations that are part of all design. To separate them from one another is artificial, since in reality there is interplay among these aspects of design and each affects the others. However, for the purpose of focusing on and emphasizing these principles, the categories will be dealt with independently. The problems are presented within the context of residential space in part because this is likely to be the kind of interior space with which you have become most familiar; at the same time, it may be that you have not yet learned to examine or plan residential interiors in an analytical and structured fashion.

1. Recipe for a Kitchen: The Effects of Line, Repetition, and Rhythm in Design

Repetition in interior design exists when there is a recurrence of some component. This could be an architectural detail, such as a specific window or columns; it could be an interior element, like the echo of a black-and-white checkered floor pattern in the wallpaper border and upholstery fabrics. Repetition in an interior can be used in many ways, but whether used with great consistency or with variations, it will act to give a sense of unity to the space.

The use of *rhythm* in an interior is related to that of repetition but implies a sense of movement. This movement can be regular as, for example, when a colored tile is installed at unvaried intervals in a long hallway floor, or irregular, as when the same colored tile is installed as the second, then the fourth, then the second, then again the fourth tile down the length of the hall. What is important in establishing rhythm is the presence of a pattern.

In design, we speak of *line* when we refer to the edges of things, to the junction of one plane with another, or the edge where a change of color, pattern, or texture takes place. Lines can be horizontal, vertical, or diagonal; they can be straight or curvilinear. In general, a room made up of horizontal lines will look serene and tranquil (like a sleeping person), while a room whose linear emphasis is vertical will appear formal and solid (like a standing person). A room with diagonals will seem lively, dramatic, and full of movement (like a running person). Curving lines in an interior suggest natural rather than man-made forms; they can provide a sense of informality that may be lacking in a space full of straight and ordered lines.

In this project, you will explore the effects of line in a kitchen interior. Using the accompanying elevation and perspective outline, which show a schematic kitchen, make colored sketches to illustrate the discussion of line in the previous paragraph. Approach your drawings as freely as possible, using inexpensive trace and pencil or marker, as well as color. Do many drawings; choose one (for each exercise described below) you like best and make a clean, clear tracing (still freehand) on vellum. You may color your original drawing on vellum, or blueprint and then color

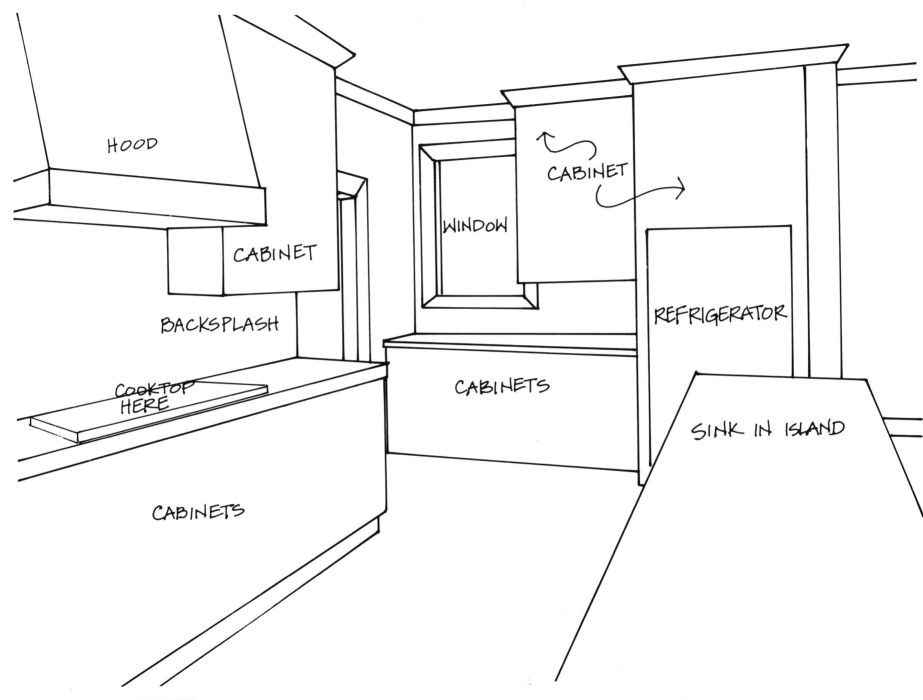

HOOD

CABINET

BACKSPLASH

COOKTOP HERE

CABINETS

WINDOW

CABINET

CABINETS

REFRIGERATOR

SINK IN ISLAND

PERSPECTIVE OF KITCHEN

it, according to instructions from your teacher.

HORIZONTAL LINES

How can you emphasize horizontal forms and lines? Some ideas are: using cabinets with horizontal boards, emphasizing the horizontal plane of the countertop by choosing a bold color, installing a continuous line of open shelves instead of upper cabinets, eliminating upper cabinets in favor of a wide window, and the use of decorative elements such as wallpaper borders, stencil designs, or a horizontal stripe along the wall between upper and lower cabinets (the backsplash area). Use some or all of these ideas, as well as any others of your own.

VERTICAL LINES

To emphasize vertical lines in this kitchen, you might use some of these techniques: installing tall upper cabinets that reach the ceiling, installing narrow upper and lower cabinets or tall, narrow windows, using vertical stripes as a decorative element, and using color to emphasize height and carry the eye upward. Use these ideas as well as your own.

DIAGONAL LINES

Although you would be unlikely to hang your cabinets at an angle to create a sense of diagonal movement (!), there are other ways to emphasize the diagonal. Your cabinets could be painted with a diagonal pattern or faced with a laminate with such a pattern. In place of conventional upper cabinets you might install custom-designed cabinets or shelves that produce a diagonal or zig-zag effect. You might create a similar effect with small windows. Decorative components, such as colors and patterns of paint, wallcovering, or tiles can be used to convey a sense of diagonal movement. What other ideas can you think of?

CURVILINEAR LINES

You have so far examined the effects of lines that are straight. How will this kitchen be affected if you now introduce curving lines? Many of the techniques already used can be adapted to this exercise. You can even try installing custom-built cabinets whose fronts undulate, or perhaps design a countertop whose edge curves gently.

FINAL PRESENTATION

When you have produced four colored drawings—one for each of the four linear categories—it will be useful for your whole class to pin up, examine, discuss, and evaluate the various solutions. Take a vote. Does the majority of your class prefer one approach over the other ones?

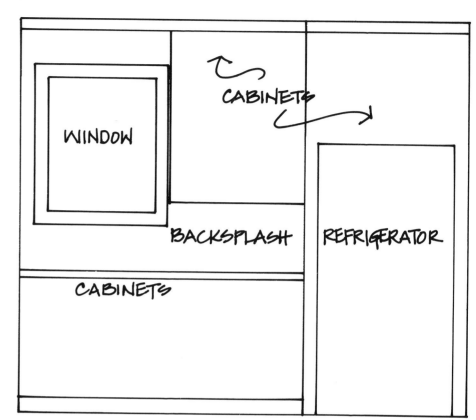

ELEVATION

Scale: ½″ = 1′-0″

2. Everything Old is New Again: Unity and Contrast

When we speak of *unity* within a design, we refer to our sense that all the parts of that design are visually connected. Some obvious examples are a monochromatic color scheme or a room filled exclusively with pieces of art and furniture of the Art Deco period. *Harmony* refers to our sense that all the elements of an interior relate to each other. The dictionary defines harmony as "a pleasing or congruent arrangement of parts," and unity as "a combination or ordering of parts in a literary or artistic production that constitutes a whole or promotes an undivided total effect." *Contrast* takes place when dissimilar elements are juxtaposed, or seen at the same time. Designers use contrast effectively to create drama, provide emphasis and create distinctions between elements in an interior. There are many ways to use contrast. In a rectangular room in which all the furniture and decorative elements are also rectangular, the presence of a large circular window will create interest and drama. In a room with a neutral color scheme, a bright red carpet will call attention to itself. If an architectural space is symmetrical, a designer might want to create an

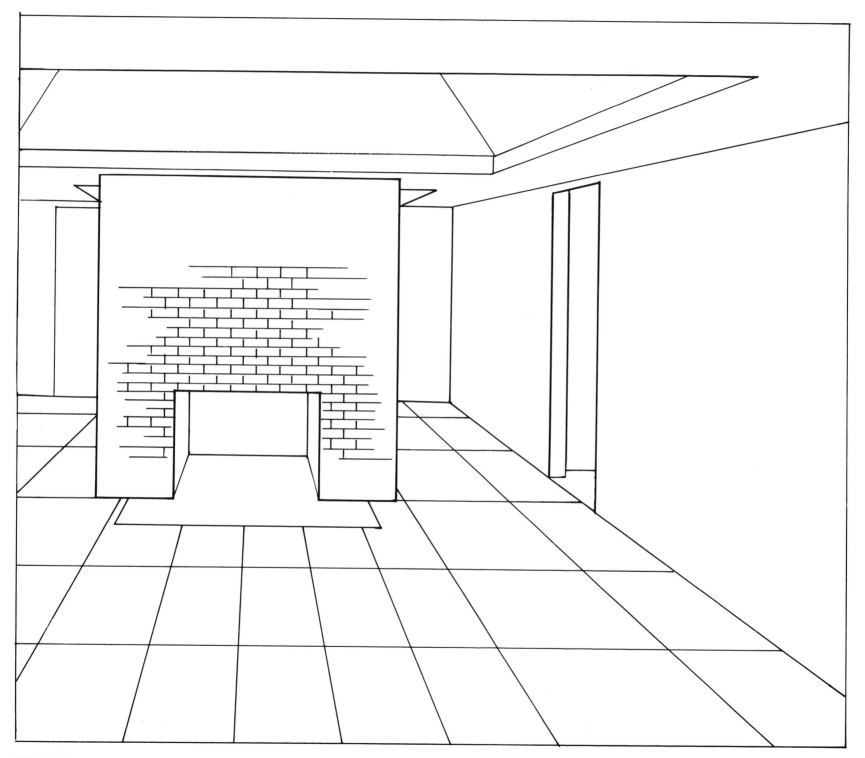

PERSPECTIVE OF LIVING ROOM

asymmetrical furniture arrangement that will capture attention.

The living room space shown in the perspective outline is contemporary. The owner has just inherited a valuable antique sofa that she is excited about. Now she has decided to redecorate the living room to include this new piece, but she needs to get rid of her old furniture. She cannot decide whether to furnish the room entirely or mostly in antiques compatible with the sofa (i.e., a unified interior) or to create a contemporary—perhaps even minimalist—interior in which the sofa is uniquely antique (an interior in which contrast is exemplified). She would like sketches showing her both of these approaches. Apart from this, she leaves all the decorating decisions up to you. You are not limited to using furniture style alone to create the desired effects; use other devices, such as line, scale, color, and so on.

In furnishing this room, consider its use. Will this room be used to entertain visitors, to watch television, or to listen to music? Will it serve all or some of these functions? Nowadays, many spacious houses have a room specifically designed for television watching, whereas a "formal" living room is reserved for conversation with guests. The ways in which you lay out your furniture will affect the use to which the room is put; for example, people wishing to talk together will want to face one another. An L-shaped or U-shaped seating arrangement, or one in which two chairs face a couch, will encourage conversation. On the other hand, if watching television is the main emphasis, the seats will be differently organized. There should probably be tables, such as coffee or end tables, for putting down cups of coffee or magazines and lamps for reading.

PRESENTATION

Using the given outline, create a rendered perspective for each of the two approaches described above.

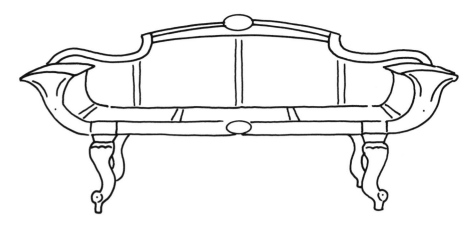

ANTIQUE SOFA: NINETEENTH-CENTURY SOFA FROM GOA, INDIA

3. Bedroom Shades: Changes in Color and Pattern

Much has been written about the uses of *color* in interior design. Many schools offer semester-long courses in color theory, in which various color systems are studied. For the purpose of completing this exercise, you do not need a lot of technical information; rather, you need to be aware of the strong impact that color has on our emotions as well as on our perception of space. Generally speaking, dark colors make a space or object look smaller, whereas light colors make them look larger. In addition, many people feel that cool colors (blues and greens) are restful, whereas warm ones (reds and yellows) are exciting. This is, however, an oversimplification. Many things affect our response to color, among them changes in fashion. For a few years, primary colors may be popular. When people tire of them, they may turn to cool mauves and grays. The trends within the fashion design world also influence those within the interior design industry. In any case, colors are rarely used in isolation but are used in juxtaposition with analogous or complementary colors.

PATTERN can be used in many ways. It can provide emphasis, as when a sofa is upholstered in a patterned material, while the rest of the room is plain. It can make something appear taller than it is, like a wall papered in vertical stripes. It can influence mood, and it is a means of introducing color.

In the following project, you are asked to explore color and pattern. As indicated above, you are not expected to know a lot about them yet. In fact, you could spend a lifetime experimenting with color and learning about it. Approach the exercise with an open mind and be adventurous in your designs!

Matthew and Nancy Doe occupy the bedroom shown in the accompanying drawing. They wish the room were larger, but they have decided not to spend any money on architectural changes to the room or to move the bed. However, they would like a new look, and they have asked you to show them what could be done using new colors and patterns. You may also show new decorative accessories, artwork, plants, and small items of furniture.

Using the perspective of the room, make color drawings that explore different decorative possibilities using paint, wallcoverings, floor coverings, and fabric. You should try different window treatments. The Does hate the bright blue carpet in this room and would like to see what the room might look like with a different kind of wall-to-wall carpet or with a wood floor (with or without an area rug). They would like one of your designs to show a monochromatic color scheme.

PRESENTATION

Three design solutions, each as different as possible from the others. For each, show the room rendered in color, using the available perspective as a starting point for your drawings.

PERSPECTIVE OF BEDROOM

4. Symmetry and Balance: A Living Room

SYMMETRY is defined as "a correspondence of size, shape, and relative position of parts on opposite sides of a dividing line . . . or center or axis." All symmetrical interiors have this centerline or axis. In a symmetrical composition, the center must be dominant, while the left and right sides are equally weighted in terms of visual emphasis.

BALANCE is defined as "an aesthetically pleasing integration of elements." The definition itself indicates how much the perception of balance is instinctive or subjective. Balance does not require symmetry, but it does require a sense of equilibrium among its elements. An asymmetrical design may appear balanced if, for instance, a large element on one side of the design is matched against several smaller elements on the other side, with each side having equal visual weight.

The accompanying drawings show you a living room space that is a large rectangle with a fireplace in the center of one wall. The purpose of this exercise is to have you examine the effects of different furniture layouts.

Build a simple foam-core board model of the space in $\frac{1}{2}'' = 1'-0''$ scale. (You may design the fireplace.) Make a list of furniture components to use as a guide and build schematic furniture in the same scale out of foam-core, cardboard, paper, or a combination of these. Now, working quickly, try a variety of symmetrical furniture arrangements. Although it may seem obvious to you that the fireplace is the focal point of the layout, this is only one possibility. Try others. A longitudinal arrangement has a dividing line or axis, whereas a radial arrangement establishes balance around a central point, like the hub of a wheel. As you complete each layout, make a quick plan and perspective sketches to record it. You will use these sketches later to analyze your layouts.

As you are designing your furniture arrangements, keep the function of the room in mind. Unless this space is used for watching television, you will want to be sure that seating is organized so that it promotes conversation. An L-shaped or U-shaped arrangement, or one that places two chairs opposite a sofa, may work well. Coffee and end tables will probably be part of the scheme. Do you want a liquor cabinet? Shelving for books or stereo?

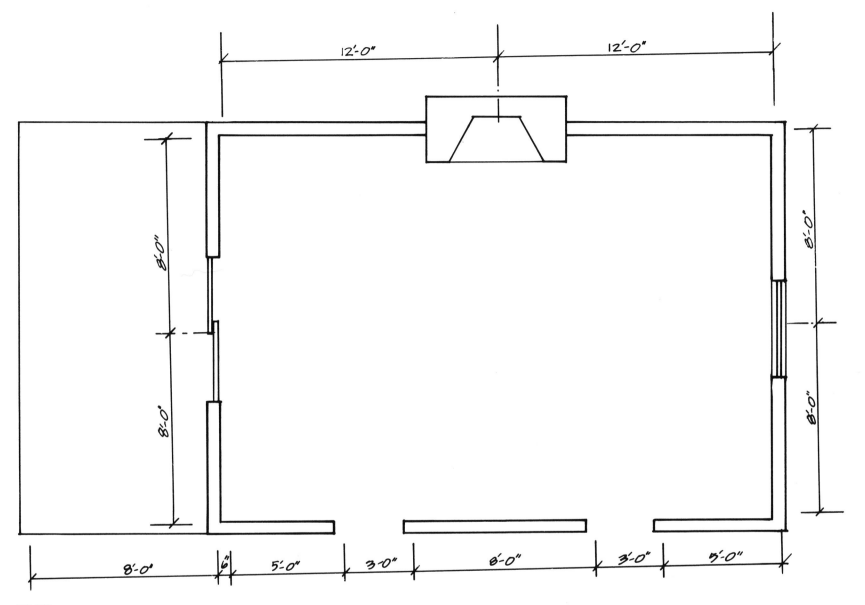

12'-0"   12'-0"

8'-0"   8'-0"

8'-0"   8'-0"

8'-0"   6"   5'-0"   3'-0"   8'-0"   3'-0"   5'-0"

PLAN

Scale: ¼″ = 1'-0″

PRESENTATION

When all members of the class have completed their sketches, the drawings can be pinned up and analyzed. What sort of feelings do these symmetrical arrangements give you? How do the radial layouts differ from the longitudinal ones?" Does one type feel more formal? More appropriate within the given space? How is traffic flow affected by the various plans?

Next, use your models and furniture components to create layouts that are asymmetrical but balanced. There are nearly endless possibilities. If you feel you need to, you may make and add other furniture or decorative elements. Once again, record your arrangements in sketches, and again, pin up sketches so that classmates may study and discuss one another's work. How do these balanced compositions affect the atmosphere of the space? Does it feel less or equally formal? How do they fit within the volume of the interior? Were they more or less easy to produce? Finally, how do you like these layouts compared with the ones that are symmetrical?

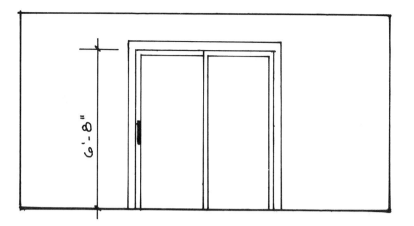

ELEVATION OF WINDOW WALL

Scale: ¼″ = 1′-0″

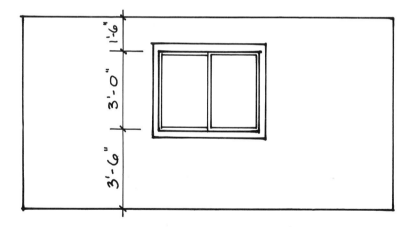

ELEVATION OF SLIDING DOORS

Scale: ¼″ = 1′-0″

5. Changes in Scale (and Size and Proportion): A Music Room

The size of an object or a space can be measured and described. Whether a room is perceived as large or small depends upon our experience and expectations; a space that would be small if used as a dining room might be considered large as a nursery or study.

SCALE is defined as "a proportion between two sets of dimensions," and this gives us a clue to its use in design. The notation of scale on a designer's drawing reveals the relationship between the size of the drawing and that of the actual space. Designers talk about the scale of objects and spaces as monumental or miniature and speak of things being "in" or "out of" scale with the things and spaces around them. The object against which all these comparisons are made is the human body. For example, if a dinner table for four is designed, it will be of a size that feels comfortable and appropriate, with respect to the distance between diners, the amount of space on the table for dinnerware, and so on. If the table is either enormous or tiny, we would say that it is "out of scale." *Anthropometrics* is the study of human body measurements, and it is this study that provides the basis for our understanding of "correct" scale.

It is important to understand, however, that scale can be manipulated to produce meaningful results. Things do not always have to be "in scale." When things are deliberately made very small or very large, in relationship to their surroundings, they have a different impact on their viewers. One simple example might be that, in a suite of offices, the door to the office of the CEO is taller than all the other doors; this extra height is noticeable and suggests the prominence of the man who occupies that office. Painters like Georgia O'Keefe, with her paintings of enormous flowers, and Andy Warhol, who painted Campbell's soup cans taller than a man, understood that to change the scale of an ordinary object is to draw attention to it. These artists were inviting viewers to look at the objects in a new way, transformed as they were from normal to monumental scale.

Architects like Michael Graves, Robert Venturi, and many others have also changed the scale of architectural components—such as columns, windows, and doors—in order to surprise us and make us take a fresh and careful look at their buildings.

Webster's dictionary defines proportion as "the harmonious relation of parts to each other or to the whole." For thousands of years, mathematicians and aestheticians have sought to establish systems for achieving ideal proportions; mostly, these theorists have attempted to explain why some things look "right," whereas others seem clearly to be out of proportion. Explanations of these systems, including the Golden Section, Palladian proportion, and Le Corbusier's Le Modulor, can be found in many books.

In this exercise, you will explore the effects of changes in size, scale, and proportion within the context of a residential space.

Matthew and Nancy Doe are professional musicians and music teachers and have decided that as they spend much of their time in their music room, they want it nicely decorated. They have asked you for advice and guidance.

The accompanying plan and sec-

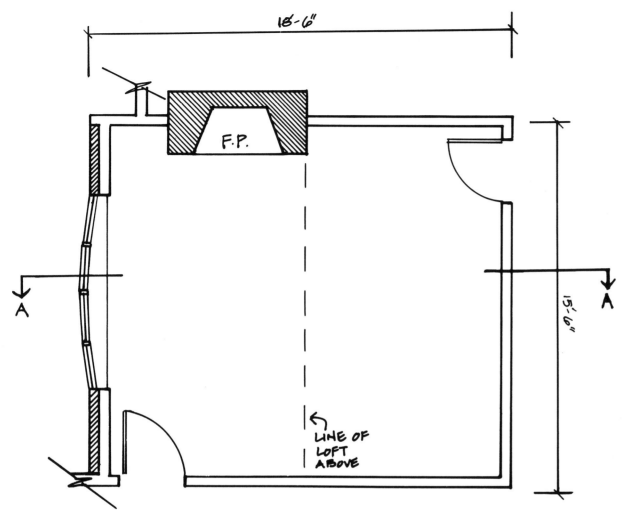

18-6"

F.P.

LINE OF
LOFT
ABOVE

15'-6"

A

A

PLAN

Scale: ¼" = 1'-0"

tion describe the space. The section shows both floors of the house; the music room is on the lower level. The Does are interested in seeing several sketches from you that explore different possibilities. They would like to know whether, given the size and scale of the room, with its high ceiling, it should be furnished with small chairs which can be moved around and grouped at will or with a large sectional (whose configuration could also be altered). Should the furniture consist of a single massive piece, several small ones, or a combination? Should the window be left without treatment, or should there be blinds, short curtains, or long drapes? Each of these approaches affects our perception of the scale and proportion of the window within this room. Experiment with color, too. This will also have an effect on our perception of the space. We know that light colors tend to make an object or space appear larger and dark colors make them smaller. How will your use of color on the walls, floors, ceilings, and furniture influence the scale and proportion of the room?

The Does have a good upright Steinway piano that they will keep, but they want to buy new furniture. They like a contemporary look and want to hang some of their abstract Neo-Expressionist

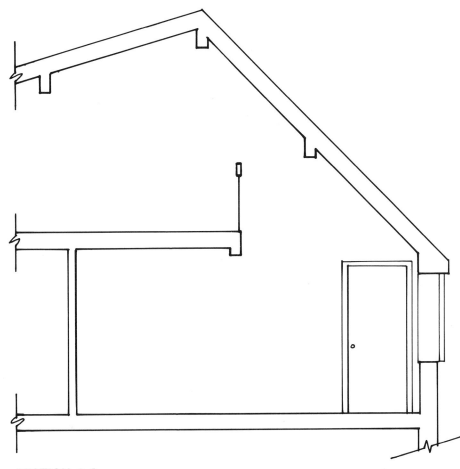

SECTION A-A

Scale: ¼″ = 1′-0″

oils in this room; they would like the colors of fabrics, paints, and floor and wall coverings to be light and neutral, so that their paintings' bold colors will dominate the space. The Does sometimes have quiet gatherings with like-minded friends who also enjoy music, so they need comfortable seating for as many people as can be reasonably fit into the space without crowding. In addition to lots of seating, they also need extensive storage for sheet music and books.

To help them visualize the different designs that you are exploring, you will construct a schematic foam-core model with simple, foam-core or cardboard furniture. Different types of furniture can be built and moved around at will.

Once you and the Does have decided on the best scheme, you will make freehand perspective sketches based on the model. (Use the model as a guide to draw from, if you are not yet familiar with the production of perspectives from plans.) While drawing, you may wish to make further changes in or additions to your designs.

PRESENTATION

Three design solutions, each described in colored perspective sketches based on the plan and section and/or on your model. One of these should show the room furnished with very large-scale pieces of furniture, one should show it furnished with a multitude of smaller scale pieces, and one with a combination of the two.

Section II
Manipulating Space

PROJECTS

6. Shaping Space with Movable Walls

7. Play Space for a Day Care Center

8. Appearances Can Be Deceptive: Making a Long Space Look Shorter

9. Living on the Outside: Designing a Backyard

10. More Than Just a Box: A Bedroom for Sisters

Whenever designers create a new space or alter an existing one, they also create or alter the user's response to that space. Imagine that you are designing a discotheque that is a big, open, high-ceilinged space. How might you want the users to perceive it? If they approach it by means of a long, low-ceilinged corridor, entering the big space might seem surprising and exciting. On the other hand, some users might find the corridor unpleasant and might be reluctant to proceed. Their experience of the same space would be quite different if they stepped directly into it from the outside. As designer, you need to try and imagine what effect your space will have on the people who use or inhabit it. Depending on the project, you will have widely varying goals. Sometimes, you may wish to surprise or excite, but at other times, you may want to create a familiar, predictable space.

You have many opportunities, as a designer, to shape space. This is true whether you practice commercial or residential interior design. You manipulate space whenever you raise or lower a ceiling or a floor, introduce a second level, install a large object that the user must walk around, or tear down walls to create a larger space. You can also manipulate space using color, pattern, or light. Remember that the act of shaping space is not done arbitrarily but with a purpose. That purpose is the creation of an interior that meets its user's functional and aesthetic needs.

The five projects that make up this section address the issue of shaping space in different ways. Some projects are commercial, some residential; one asks you to design exterior space, another requires that you explore the effects of designing on two levels. One project requires you to think about the use of "negative" space. All of them, however, demand that you consider the ways in which your design choices affect the user's physical and psychological perceptions.

You and five other designers have decided, after several years of working in large architectural firms, to establish an interior design business of your own. You plan to lease space within an old industrial building in downtown Boston. Because you want to keep build-out costs to a minimum, you intend to assemble workstations with partial height, movable walls and to leave the rest of the space open. The purpose of this project is to explore the ways in which your arrangement of the workstations affects the "leftover" space.

The floor plan and elevation show the space, with its wall of windows and the location of the entrance. An axonometric and a plan show a typical workstation (they are all the same). Where you locate the workstations within the 4,000-square-foot space is up to you, and how you place them will determine what the remaining, open space looks and feels like. For example, if all the stations are lined up along one wall, the rest of the space will be rectangular; however, if the stations are laid out in a U-shaped configuration, then they will create a smaller, enclosed rectangle

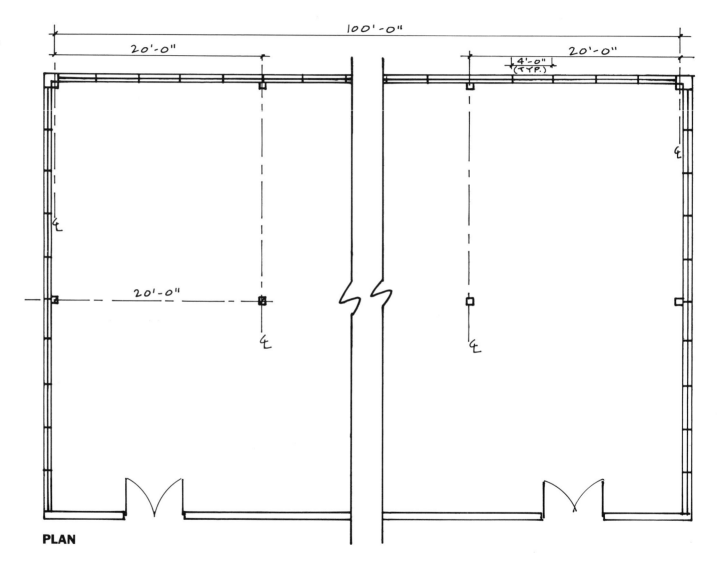

PLAN

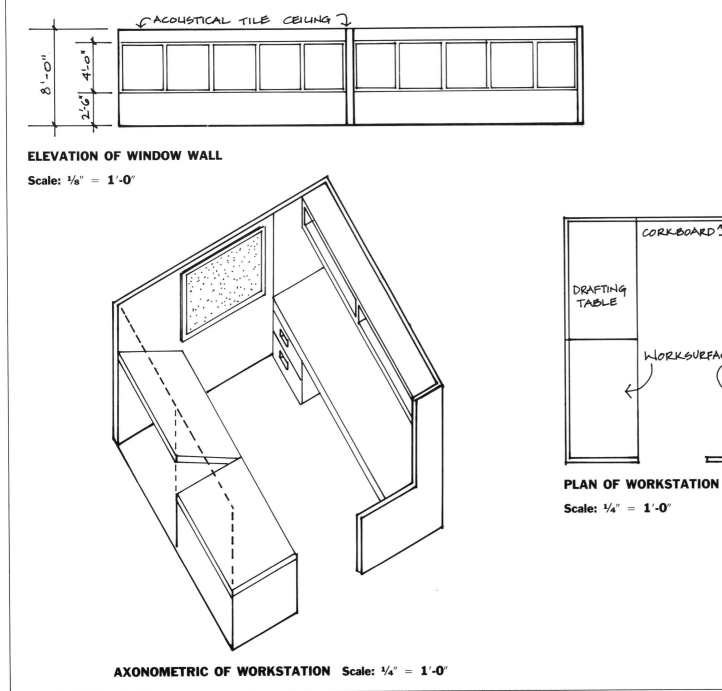

ACOUSTICAL TILE CEILING

8'-0"
4'-0"
2'-6"

ELEVATION OF WINDOW WALL

Scale: ⅛″ = 1'-0″

AXONOMETRIC OF WORKSTATION **Scale:** ¼″ = 1'-0″

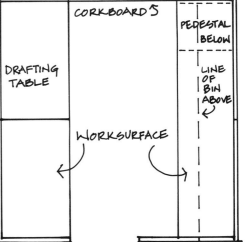

CORKBOARD

PEDESTAL BELOW

DRAFTING TABLE

LINE OF BIN ABOVE

WORKSURFACE

PLAN OF WORKSTATION

Scale: ¼″ = 1'-0″

within the larger space. This smaller space could function as a reception or conference area, or a file "room."

You and your colleagues have decided that you will need the following:

Six workstations, 10' × 10'.
Reception area to seat 4, near entrance, attractively furnished with art, display of your work, planters, etc.
Conference area furnished with a table, 4' × 8', with six chairs, and a storage unit, 6' wide × 2' deep × 6' tall, in which to keep audio-visual equipment.
Equipment: a blueprint machine, 30" wide × 24" deep, sitting on a cabinet of the same dimensions that holds blueprint paper. This should be placed as far from human activity as feasible as it emits fumes during operation. Flat files, 48" wide × 30" deep, near blueprint machine. Worktable, 36" wide × 24" deep, near blueprint machine. Worktable, 48" × 24" deep, to hold table-top copier and fax machine, with small refrigerator, 19" wide, beneath. Lateral files: three, each 42" wide × 18" deep. Storage cabinet, 36" wide × 18" deep, for miscellaneous supplies.
Samples: Wherever convenient, you will need to show shelves, 18" deep, to hold the many catalogs,

sample carpet and wallcovering books, boxes of laminate chips and so on, which will accumulate over time. Show as many of these shelves as you can.

Your solution to this design problem will develop in the following way: first, each member of the class will make a very schematic cardboard-and-tape model of the workstation, showing just the walls and entrance, in ¼" scale. This model only needs to last for a short time and need not be very durable.

Next, members of the class will assemble in groups of (ideally) six. One member of each group will quickly sketch the floor plan at ¼" scale; the little workstation models will be placed on this plan.

For the next thirty minutes, each "team" will group six workstations on the plan in as many ways as possible: longitudinally, diagonally, in zig-zag fashion, and so on. As you complete each grouping, discuss the effect each layout has on the overall space and how you might be able to arrange the reception, conference, and equipment areas in the leftover space. Make notes and thumbnail sketches as you go. You should plan to produce at least 6 different arrangements in a half-hour.

Next, you will resume working as

individuals. Each of you will select the three arrangements you liked best and proceed to develop them further.

PRESENTATION FOR EACH ARRANGEMENT:

Floor plan: ¼" = 1'-0" scale, on vellum. Show not only the workstation layout, but also the furniture and equipment layouts within the reception, conference and equipment areas.

7. Play Structure for a Day Care Center

Your client is Kidspace, a day care center located in a mall in a southern California city. The center is owned by Rob and Molli Righter. Business is good, and the Righters will open at least one more center in another part of the city.

To celebrate the grand opening of the second Kidspace, the Righters are renovating the original center. Most of the renovation involves painting and the installation of new flooring, which the Righters are overseeing. However, they called you in to design a play structure or structures that will occupy a large portion of the interior.

The purpose of this play structure is twofold. First, it is to be appealing to children and to provide them with lots of exercise! Second, it is a place within which children will engage in group play; therefore, you should provide little "rooms" and platforms where groups of four or five children can assemble. In addition, and just as important, the Righters want the structure to enhance the overall space. The rest of the interior will be finished simply and with neutral colors, so you can and should make the structure as fanciful and colorful as possible. This is a big object that will have tremendous visual impact and be a focal point within the Kidspace interior. You should use shapes and colors that are lively, dramatic, and fun! These shapes may be abstract, representational, or a combination of both. In addition, the structure should be safe and sturdy, and the children must be able to climb on, in, under, and through it.

Above all, consider the ways in which your design affects the surrounding space. If the structure is circular, the path around it may also be irregular. Because it is so large, its materials and colors—bright? shiny? multicolored or monochromatic?—will also affect the users' perception of the rest of the interior.

The accompanying plan shows the interior of the space and the desired size and location of the structure. Note that the height to the bottom of the floor above is 14'-0", and the suspended ceiling may be hung at any height up to 12'-0". The Righters would like the structure to be built primarily of wood, which is inexpensive and can be painted; they have also indicated that you can incorporate other materials—such as PVC pipe or fire-resistant fabric—if you wish.

PRESENTATION

Colored model built of foam-core board in 1' = 1'-0" scale. (You should provide a small figure in the same scale to give a sense of the structure's size. In addition, use large pieces of foam-core board or cardboard to represent the floor and walls of the entire space. Place your model and scale figure within this environment.)

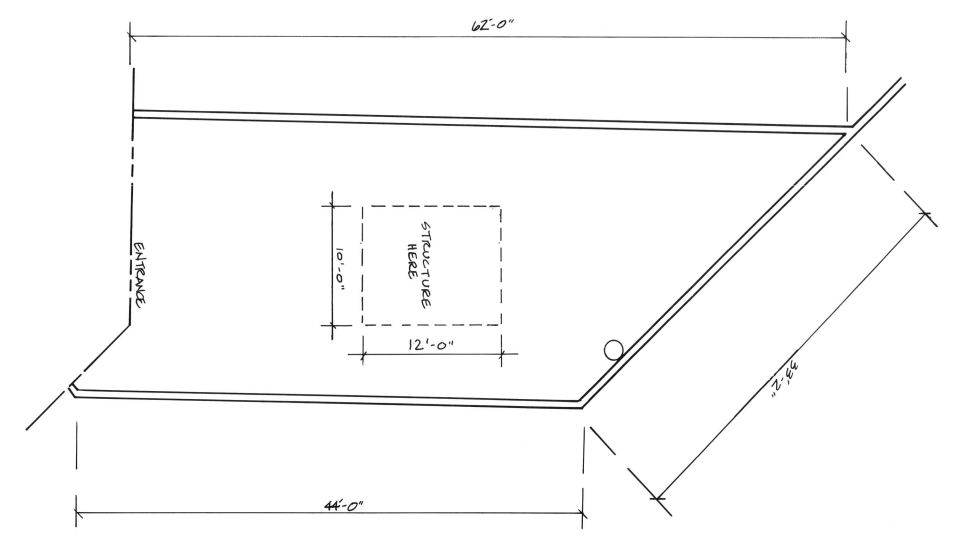

62'-0"

ENTRANCE

STRUCTURE HERE

10'-0"

12'-0"

33'-2"

44'-0"

PLAN

Scale: ⅛″ = 1′-0″

Arthur Smith has finally decided to quit his job as an assistant district attorney in order to pursue a dream: opening his own art gallery. After much consideration, he has decided to combine it with a café that serves Italian coffees and Viennese pastries (but that has no kitchen). The requirements for food service and for a handicapped-accessible bathroom are simple; both are located at the back of the space and are shown on the accompanying plan and section/elevation.

The remainder of the space will accommodate 30"-diameter tables with chairs and display of art-works. You will determine the appropriate number of tables when you lay out the space. Whereas paintings will be hung on the walls, sculptures will be displayed on eight movable pedestals, each 18" square × 36" high.

The problem Mr. Smith faces, and which he has hired you to solve, is that of making what is actually a very long and narrow space appear less tunnel-like, a problem faced by many retail operations. Mr. Smith has leased space in a nineteenth-century brick building with party walls and only one window at the front. This space is shown in the plan and section/elevation.

It will help you, in preparing to solve this problem, to visit some mall stores and others that have a long and narrow configuration and see how some of them have dealt with it. You will find that some stores ignore the problem and that others find solutions. These may include the introduction of diagonal or curvilinear objects or aisles, placement of ceiling or floor tiles perpendicular or diagonal to the long axis of the space, breaking a long space into a series of smaller ones, the manipulation of lighting and ceiling design to affect perception of the space, or the use of color and pattern to interrupt the sense of a long interior space. There will certainly be other techniques not listed here, and you will probably feel that some are more effective than others.

Your solution will begin with quick sketches. First, create two perspective outlines of the space, one looking toward the back, the other toward the front. You will use these outlines to make the different ideas similar to those described in the preceding paragraph. Use cheap trace and a variety of media. At this stage of schematic design, do not worry about details like accurate placement of tables or pedestals; rather, try to get a more general sense of the space as it is affected by your solutions.

When you have finished several quick sketches, study them and make decisions concerning those approaches which you find successful. You will incorporate these into your final solution.

PRESENTATION

Model: 1/4" = 1' minimum scale, made of foam-core board, with color and pattern indicated as accurately as possible. (It is not necessary to construct the part of the space occupied by bathroom and food service.) Your furniture, pedestals, and other items can also be made of foam-core. The ceiling should be removable, so that the space can be viewed from above. However, a more realistic view of the interior, and one that gives a better indication of your success, is obtained by looking through the front windows—particularly if you have created a ceiling whose design significantly affects the space.

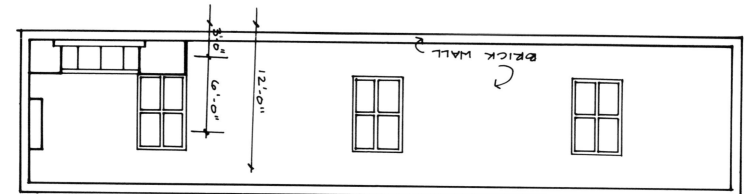

ELEVATION

Scale: ⅛" = 1'-0"

BRICK WALL

3'-0"
6'-0"
12'-0"

PLAN

Scale: ⅛" = 1'-0"

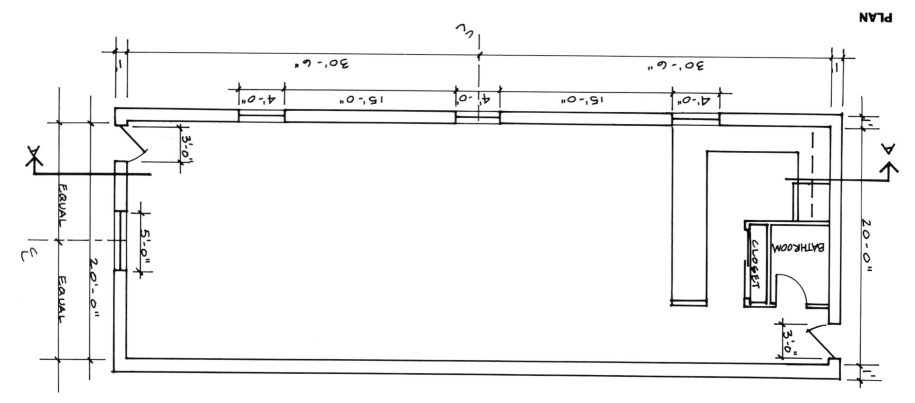

30'-6"
4'-0" 15'-0" 4'-0" 15'-0" 4'-0"
30'-6"

EQUAL
EQUAL
20'-0"
5'-0"
3'-0"

20'-0"
3'-0"

BATHROOM
CLOSET

9. Living on the Outside: Designing a Backyard

Although you probably don't think of interior designers as landscape architects—and, of course, they do not get the same training—it is true that all designers, whether architects, landscape architects, or interior designers, need to consider similar issues. Therefore, though this project seems at first glance to be a landscaping problem, it is really about the manipulation of space in a more general way. The outdoor space that you are about to design will require some walls, some "ceiling," "flooring," color, and pattern—in short, most of the characteristics of interior space. Above all, it will require you to think about the visual and functional separation of spaces and about the ambiance that your many choices create.

The accompanying plan and elevation show the yard and back of the nineteenth-century townhouse that Fred and Bea Potter have just bought in Washington, D.C.'s, historic Georgetown district. Lived in for some years by a man who spent much of his time travelling, its backyard has been ill tended and is now overgrown with weeds.

The Potters have an eight-year-old son and a two-year-old daughter. They have decided that the yard should be organized so that there is a play space for the children at the back (the alley end), whereas the area that abuts the house will be developed as an area with comfortable seating and a table for outdoor meals. You should note that there are several steps leading from the kitchen door down into the yard. Thus, the seating area can be at the level of the kitchen—on a deck with steps leading down into the garden—or on the same level as the yard. The Potters are leaving this decision up to you.

Fred and Bea have asked you to pay particular attention, as you design, to providing some visual separation between the eating area and the play area; however, they do not want their view of the children obscured.

These, then, are their requirements.

1. *Play area* for kids at the back, which could include any combination of the following: swing set, play structure, playhouse, sandbox. A small storage shed for toys, bikes, etc. would be desirable.

2. *Seating/dining area* near the house. This *must* be shaded, since Washington summers can be hot. It would take too long to grow a big shade tree, so you will have to design a structure that covers this whole space. Possibilities include a superstructure made of wood alone or of wood used in combination with canvas strips (what an opportunity for using color!), fiberglass panels, vines growing on an arbor, etc. Remember that the pattern you create in this overhead structure will affect that of the shadows it casts and is itself an important design element.

3. *A tall fence* all around the yard—with a gate opening into the alley—to give privacy and security. Materials you might use include: wood (many different designs), wrought iron, concrete block (again, many patterns are available), stone, brick, etc.

4. *A path or paved area* connecting the different parts of the garden. Materials used here could be wood, stone, brick, railroad ties, cut logs, concrete, or a combination.

5. *Planters and planted areas:* Remember that these define and shape space just as much as walls or pieces of furniture. Fred Potter says, "No grass, please!"

6. *Some water:* Bea insists on this.

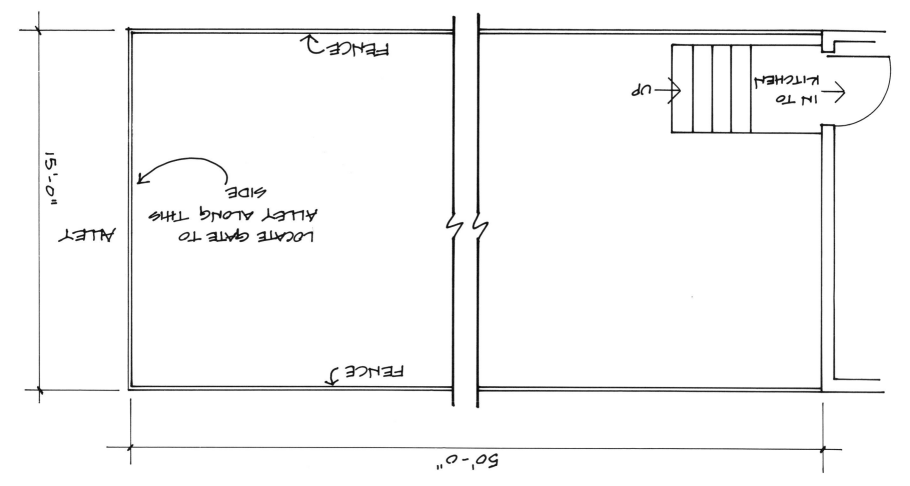

BACKYARD PLAN

Scale: ¼″ = 1′-0″

FENCE

FENCE

LOCATE GATE TO
ALLEY ALONG THIS
SIDE

ALLEY

15′-0″

50′-0″

UP →

IN TO
KITCHEN →

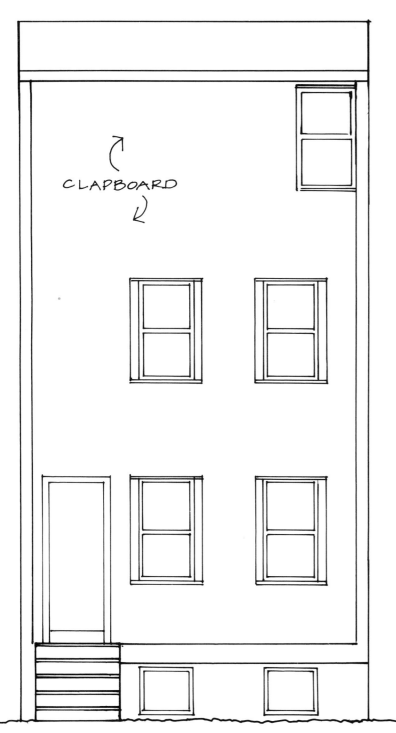

CLAPBOARD

ELEVATION   Scale: ¼″ = 1′-0″

But a very small pond will do.

7. *A little shed*—4′ × 4′ would be adequate—for garden tools. It could be built against the house, or fence, or could be freestanding.

Above all, the Potters want an *interesting* design, one that is enticing and exciting. What does this mean? It may mean that, if you create a path leading toward the back, it will curve or meander. It may mean that there will be little, secret, sheltered areas (like little rooms) that you create. Don't forget that the means to the end in this project are fences and foliage rather than couches and curtains—but that you are developing a space for living, just the same.

PRESENTATION

Model: ½″ = 1′-0″ minimum scale. Build as much as possible out of foam-core board. Use a sheet of foam-core to represent the back wall of the house, with the details of windows and door drawn on. Some art-supply stores sell materials for use in representing plants for model-builders, but you can probably invent your own, using whatever materials are at hand. Make the textures and colors of your design as accurate as possible.

10. More Than Just a Box: A Room for Sisters

Your parents have just purchased a large portion of an old mill on a canal. They are allotting a section of it to you to design as a bed/study/entertainment room that you will share with your sister or brother. The available space is shown in the plan and elevation.

The ceiling is high enough that you can and should design your room on more than one level. Consider one or more loft spaces. Think about access to the upper level(s); will it be by ladder or by stairs, and if by stairs, will they be a straight or curved run, or spiral? Think about the possibility of creating platforms, of dropping the ceiling in some sections of the space. This is an opportunity to think about space in a sculptural way. Don't simply produce a "shoebox" or doll's house into which you stuff pieces of furniture! In addition, you should think about color and pattern as they enhance architectural form. (For instance, if your space were bisected by a zig-zag wall, you might want that wall alone to be painted a brilliant red, which would draw attention to it.)

This project will be completed in several stages, which are described below.

1. *Programming.* You should consider your separate and shared needs. Will you want bunk beds or separate spaces for sleeping? Should study spaces be together or apart? Will there be a TV or stereo? How much space should be allotted to storage for clothes, for books, or for specialized collections? Do either of you have need of some less usual provision—for instance, a ballet barre and mirror? You should make a list of all your requirements. Make some general decisions about the layout of the different functions within the room.

2. *Sketching.* You will now begin to make some rough sketches; you will need to do not only plans, but also elevations and sections, in order to make good design decisions. Your drawings at this stage should be very loose.

3. *Sketch model.* When enough of your design has been determined that you can produce a model, you should make a quick one of foam-core board and/or heavy cardboard, in $\frac{1}{2}'' = 1'\text{-}0''$ scale. The purpose of this model is to allow you, your classmates and your teacher to take

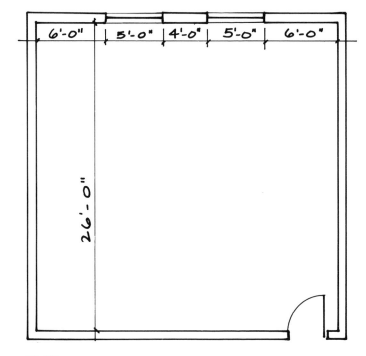

PLAN

Scale: $\frac{1}{8}'' = 1'\text{-}0''$

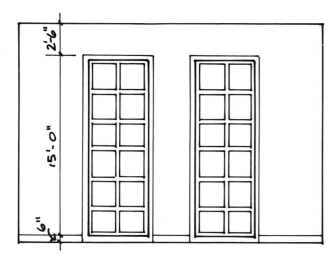

ELEVATION OF WINDOW WALL

Scale: ⅛″ = **1′-0″**

a look at your design direction and to think about modifications.

4. *Final presentation:* Foam-core model in ½″ = 1′-0″ scale. Furniture should be fairly schematic and may be entirely built of foam-core. The model should be colored. Large expanses of solid color are best done with Color-Aid paper glued to the foam-core. This is quick and neat. In addition, provide a plan and a section in ½″ = 1′-0″ scale, rendered in color.

Section III
Programming

PROJECTS

Programming is one of the most important elements in the planning of a project. It is a complete, written list of project requirements and can be prepared either before or after the selection of a site.

To write a program, you need to interview your client(s). This may mean talking to a single individual or to the department heads within a company. Begin by preparing a general project statement that outlines the purpose of the design project. Next, analyze the proposed use of the space. For example, will it be used by one or many people? What are the living habits of the tenants? If it is an office space, ask which employees communicate most frequently with others, so that you can establish a list of adjacencies. Which ones must be on a window wall? You need to list the various spaces required, their proposed sizes, their functions, and their contents. You will need to list every aspect of the project, including such things as the need for privacy, lighting requirements, color preferences, storage needs, and so on.

Your program may be subject to revision, either during the initial interview or later in the design process. You may discover that your client seems to change his mind about his requirements after he sees your initial sketches or plans. This can happen because the client is not in the habit of analyzing his needs and has not thought carefully about the way he really lives or works. When he sees the plan, however, he then perceives that it will not function exactly as he had expected and that he forgot to mention something in his early interviews with you! Your program, however, is still a necessary guide to planning. Without it, your approach to a design problem is simply guesswork.

11. A Place for Trace: Creating a Home Studio

This project will proceed in several steps; you will be required to design both individually and as a member of a team, as you program, space-plan and select materials.

Imagine that you must create a studio space where you are living, a place to work on your design projects. This might be in the corner of a bedroom—whether in a dorm room or house—in a closet converted to this purpose, in a portion of an attic or basement, or any other place that is appropriate and realistic.

Before you decide where you will put this studio, you must make a list of everything it will accommodate. This list is part of your program. Think about materials that must be stored: trace, vellum, markers, triangles, books, and so on. Think about the drawing surface: will you have a portable drawing board or a drafting table? Consider including a surface, perhaps a worktable or counter, for miscellaneous work such as model building or making presentation boards, which involves the use of glue and a utility knife. Perhaps you would like a bulletin or tack

board on which you can hang notes, reminders, clippings from magazines or work in progress. Your program should also note all of your requirements; for instance, you should write down the size of the drafting board, the number of linear feet of shelving required, number of drawers or other storage space, size of tack board if included, and so on. As you make this list, you can be thinking about the possibilities for locating the studio.

Once you have determined the location, measure the room and existing furniture and prepare a floor plan, with existing furniture layout, drawn to scale. Make notes on the plan of window sill and ceiling heights. If the room has a sloping ceiling, dormers, or any irregularities, you will also need to prepare a section and/or elevation.

In the next part of this project, you will be the client in the design of your own studio space and the designer in the development of another student's space. Exchange programs and floor plans with a classmate. Each of you will proceed to design the workspace for the other, using the program as a

guide and checklist. Since you are handing the job of designing this space to someone else, your program must be complete and your drawings accurate.

PRESENTATION

Floor plan, sections and elevations as required to describe final design. Scale: ¼″ = 1′-0″.

If you design special storage units, such as built-in shelves, cabinets, files, and so on, you may need to draw sections or elevations of these units at a larger scale.

College campuses have many offices that have become cluttered, overcrowded, and inefficient. Often, this is because the office was originally intended to house fewer employees or less equipment, and over time, people, desks, cabinets, copiers (and so on) have been added. Typically, such offices have a multitude of mismatched work surfaces, inadequate storage (cardboard boxes are shoved under tables), and poorly designed circulation patterns. Furniture is arranged haphazardly, and people are almost tripping over one another as they try to function in the space.

Take a walk around your campus and find an office that both you and the employees who use it agree functions poorly and is badly organized in the ways described above. Look for a space of between approximately 250 and 350 square feet, one that accommodates several people. You will redesign this office.

The first step in solving your design program is to understand fully the space. Interview the employees and record every one of their complaints about their work environment. Observe them at work for thirty minutes on one or two occasions to document any additional problems in its organization that they may not have identified. You will also need to ask the employees to give you their "wish lists," which might include such unrelated things as additional storage for books, a place for informal conferences, more individual privacy, or a nicer paint color on the walls! Study the space and make notes of your own criticisms (having to do with function or aesthetics) and suggestions. The list of both problems and desired changes must be complete and organized on paper: this is the program.

Next, measure the room, including window sill and ceiling heights, and all the existing furniture. It is likely that you will have to accomplish your ends using the existing furniture. However, if you are clever about utilizing what is there and about designing additional storage space (like built-in closets or wall-hung shelves and cabinets), you may be able to eliminate some awkward pieces of furniture, thereby freeing up floor space for better traffic flow. Draw the plan at ¼″ = 1′-0″ scale.

The third step in the process is the production of a schematic design. This can be accomplished in many ways, but the goal is to explore as many variations as possible in the arrangement of furniture. You might like to try drawing the furniture at ¼″ scale, cutting out the pieces and moving them around on the plan. Be sure, however, that this does not inhibit you in proposing solutions that do not use the existing furniture, such as the installation of a long built-in counter.

Once you have determined your layout and solved any other design problems on your list, you will make a final drawing that can be given to your "clients." In this final drawing, you may need to refine design details and provide notes to clarify your intentions.

PRESENTATION

Floor plan, including furniture layout and notes as required concerning construction or materials: ¼″ = 1′-0″ scale.

Elevations as needed to describe design: ¼″ = 1′-0″ scale.

13. California or Bust: Planning Your First Condo

Let's imagine that you have finished your study of interior design and have accepted an offer of a job with a design firm in San Francisco.

While looking for a place to live, you discover that part of an old building near the Embarcadero is to be converted to condominiums. If you act quickly, before all the units are finished, you will be able to design your own unit (with a few exceptions).

You decide to purchase a lovely unit with tall windows overlooking the Golden Gate Bridge. The plan and elevation show the space at the time of purchase. The bathroom is already built, and the location of the plumbing in the kitchen is established. It is up to you to design the kitchen and everything else you need.

You will begin by writing a program—a complete and specific list of all your requirements. Start by deciding how many different functions the space will perform—for instance, living area, sleeping, dining, and working. Will these require separate or shared spaces? The living room couch could open

into a bed, a Murphy bed could be concealed in a closet, a rolled-up futon could serve as a bed on the floor, or you might choose to create a bedroom behind full-height walls or shoji screens. You will definitely need to provide space for working at home from time to time; thus, you could set up a drafting table, have a portable board that can be put away, or you could build a work counter (which might even double as a dining table). The possibilities are not really endless, but there are a great many options. For each area, make a detailed list of every item to be accommodated. Be sure to include all the necessary storage space—for clothes, books, blueprints, drawing equipment, and so on, and remember that a list must also be made up for the kitchen.

When you have completed your program, begin the planning process by creating bubble diagrams for the major areas. This is the point at which you will decide which areas are adjacent to the windows and which are interior. You should try several different layouts. Once you have a general idea of the locations of the various spaces, begin to refine your draw-

ing, so that you are giving form to the areas; it is at this stage that you will want to experiment with the placement of walls—full height, partial height, perhaps with windows inserted that admit borrowed light into an interior space; you may decide that the entire space should be open, with no partitions except for those that enclose the bathroom. A further refinement takes place when you do your furniture layout. At this point, you may find that you need to adjust the spaces, to give more square footage to one area and less to another.

PRESENTATION

Floor plan at $\frac{1}{2}'' = 1'-0''$ scale, showing all partitions, kitchen layout and furniture layout. The plan should be clearly labeled, with plenty of notes to describe the provisions made for storage.

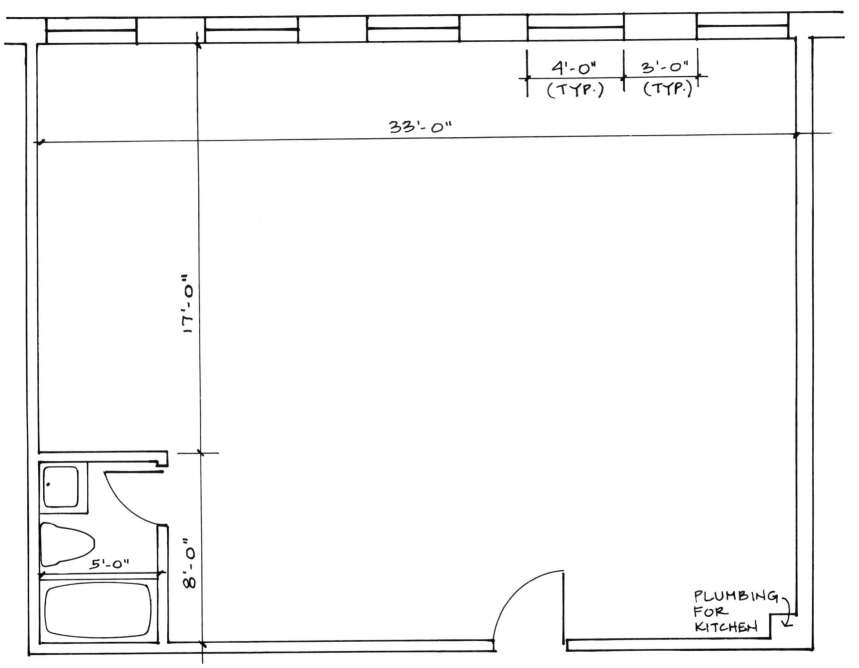

4'-0"
(TYP.)

3'-0"
(TYP.)

33'-0"

17'-0"

8'-0"

5'-0"

PLUMBING
FOR
KITCHEN

PLAN

Scale: ¼″ = **1'-0″**

ELEVATION OF WINDOW WALL

Scale: ¼″ = **1′-0″**

14. Fun in the Sun: A Place of Your Own

WRITING A PROGRAM

You have just inherited money from a distant cousin—not a great deal, but enough to build the little getaway place you have always dreamed of! This project begins with your wish list.

If you had a small place of your own, what would you most like? Some possibilities include: a cabin in ski country, a house on the beach, a place in the woods to use for meditation, or a little studio in which to do ceramics, painting, photography, or other activity you find relaxing and recreational. You may visualize this place as one that is yours alone—to get away from people—or one that is shared by family or friends. Keep in mind, however, that 700 square feet (the maximum space allowed) is not enough space to accommodate many people in separate bedrooms, so if you plan to bring many children or others to stay in your place, you will need to come up with some innovative ideas for sleeping arrangements.

Your place should be no smaller than 400 and no larger than 700 square feet. There are no other re-strictions. You may imagine it placed on any site you like, in any part of the world.

Write a program so complete that another designer or architect could design the project in your absence. This means that you need to de-scribe the purpose of the place, its site, every item it must include, and any requirements you have concerning furniture, finish mate-rials, lighting, ambience, and style. Do not forget that, as you enumerate the rooms and contents of the house, you need to keep track of its size, making sure you do not exceed the square footage allowed.

SCHEMATIC DESIGN AND DESIGN DEVELOPMENT

If you go on to the second phase of this project, you will spend two class periods (at least five or six hours) exploring possibilities for the layout of your place and the design of its exterior. You need to draw all four exterior elevations, as well as the floor plan, sections, and perspective sketches to describe your design. When you sketch the exterior, consider the purpose of the building, so that you can make the design of the exterior reflect its use. If it is to be a retreat for med-itation, perhaps you will design it with a roof that suggests that of Japanese temples. You may wish to make it open to the outdoors, with walls of glass that overlook a stream or woods, so that the med-itator feels "in touch" with the en-vironment. If it is to be a study for a writer, on the other hand, a building shutting out its surround-ings in order to eliminate distrac-tions might be desirable. In this case, there might be few windows, and the exterior could be either very plain or could be decorated with paint or with architectural motifs.

Do your initial drawings freehand, using your scale, if necessary, but not your T-square and triangle. Work quickly toward a solution. Keep it fairly simple. By the end of the allotted time, you should have reached final decisions con-cerning all aspects of the designs of interior and exterior.

You are now ready to expand upon and refine your design. As you begin to create scaled drawings, you will undoubtedly make further changes in your design; this is a natural part of design development. (Note: make quick sketch models of paper or cardboard, if you have problems visualizing your house or some part of it, such as the roof.)

PRESENTATION

Floor plan, four exterior elevations, one perspective sketch, and sections as needed to explain your design. All drawings may be on rough trace and may be freehand. Scale: $\frac{1}{2}'' = 1'-0''$

THE MODEL

If you go on to the third phase of this project, you will build a model of your dream getaway house. Building the model allows you to get a better sense of your design and to analyze it with greater accuracy. The model should be made of foam-core board, with schematic furniture (which may also be made of foam-core board) shown. Colors may be indicated with the use of Color-Aid paper, construction paper, markers or colored pencil, or other media. The roof of the house should be able to be lifted off so that the interior may be better viewed. Scale: $\frac{1}{2}'' = 1'-0''$

15. A Permanent Home for a Hair Salon: Part 1

This project is made up of several parts: programming, space-planning, and furniture and finish selection.

Jerri has been operating a hairdressing establishment out of her home in suburban Connecticut for two years. She now has a loyal clientele that is large enough that she needs more space and assistants. She has decided to lease part of a small outdoor mall in town; the space is inexpensive, very well located, and adequate for her needs. She has provided you with a plan, exterior elevation, interior elevation, and exterior perspective.

Jerri has hired you to plan and design the place and would like your advice concerning the number of stations the space can accommodate, how to incorporate an area for a manicurist, whether she should include an employee lounge, and so on. She also wants you to come up with an exciting design scheme. Jerri has borrowed quite a bit of money to open this salon. She is a risk taker, something of a flamboyant character, well known among her customers as innovative, daring, a "character." She wants all this to be reflected in the ambience of the place.

Begin by visiting one or two hair salons near you. Interview the managers and obtain a *complete* list of everything contained in the salons. You must be sure to get information concerning the size of the individual stations and the components that make up each station, the size of the hair-washing area, the requirements for an area where coloring takes place, the size and components of the reception area (which may also be where hair and beauty products are sold), nonpublic areas such as an office or employee lounge, bathrooms, storage for towels, shampoo, coats, and so on, and any other areas that the people you interview might name. Organize all the information into a list that identifies all the items and spaces needed in a hair salon. You will use this list to design a place for Jerri and show her what she can accommodate in her new space.

Now that you have completed a program, you will begin space-planning. Important: you may locate the main entrance wherever you like. Also note that building code requires a second means of egress located as far as possible from the main entry and unobstructed by furniture or interior doors. In this portion of the project, you are attempting to discover exactly how many stations can fit into the designated area after all other needs—for bathrooms, reception, storage, and so on—have been met. Keep in mind that although some hair salons are very crowded, Jerri wants her place to be rather elegant, so the stations should not be too close together. Using your bubble or block diagramming techniques, make some quick sketches to find out how best to organize the space. Think, as you are experimenting with different layouts, about what should be visible through the big windows from the street; this is a retail business and may attract some walk-in trade. As you are working on your space-planning, you should be thinking about finishes, colors, furniture, lighting, and decoration. You should be thinking about the image Jerri wants this interior to project, an image that expresses her character and the character of the business. These considerations may affect decisions you make concerning the layout of stations, design of the reception area, circulation patterns, and other aspects of the plan.

When your rough space-planning has been done, you will refine your

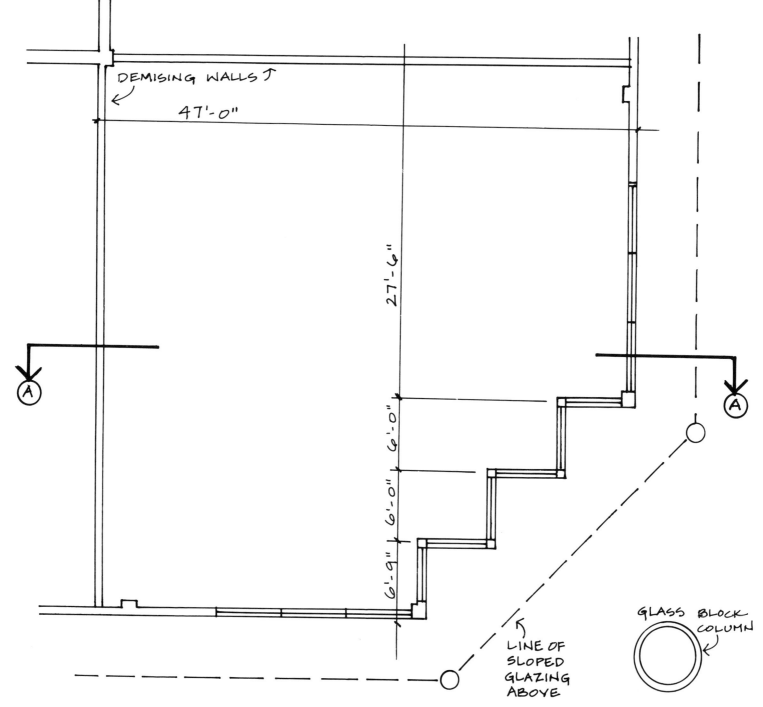

DEMISING WALLS ↑

47'-0"

27'-6"

6'-0"

6'-0"

6'-9"

A

A

LINE OF
SLOPED
GLAZING
ABOVE

GLASS BLOCK
COLUMN

PLAN Scale: ⅛″ = 1'-0″

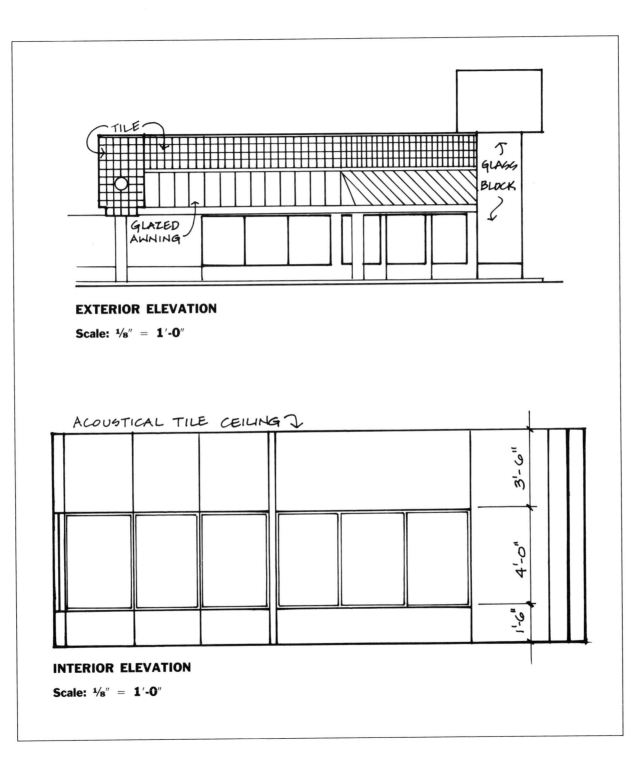

EXTERIOR ELEVATION

Scale: ⅛″ = 1′-0″

INTERIOR ELEVATION

Scale: ⅛″ = 1′-0″

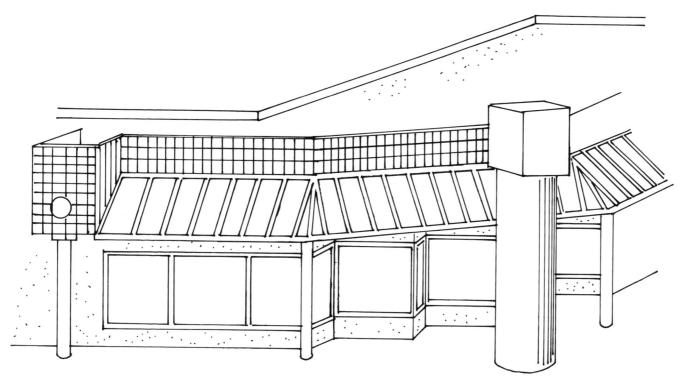

EXTERIOR PERSPECTIVE

layout, making sure that all details are accounted for. Will there be one coat closet for visitors near reception and another for employees in a back room? Are the entrances to the bathrooms discreetly placed? Have you provided a handicapped-accessible bathroom?

After the plan is completed, you will need to refine your selections of finishes, color, furniture, and so on. Because all aspects of a design relate to one another, you may find at this stage that you still make some adjustments to the layout.

PRESENTATION

Floor plan, rendered in color: ¼″ = 1′-0″ scale.

Reflected ceiling plan: ¼″ = 1′-0″ scale.

Axonometric, rendered in color: ¼″ = 1′-0″ scale.

Significant materials, such as carpet, wallcovering, and fabrics, should be shown and can be attached, appropriately labeled, to the plan or axonometric.

Section IV

Space-Planning

PROJECTS

16. Make Space for Our Place: Offices for an Accounting Firm

17. Keep an Open Mind: Open Plan Office

18. Doctor, Doctor: Planning to Meet the Needs of Several Clients

19. Which Way In? Alternative Layouts for Offices

20. Develop Plans for a Developer

"SPACE-PLANNER" is a term frequently used to describe designers who specialize in the layout of offices or systems furniture. These designers may be asked to plan the layout of partitions within the open, undivided space of an office building or to provide drawings showing clients the best possible configuration of furniture for open office plans. In fact, space-planning skills are used whenever interior design takes place. They are required when an apartment or condominium is planned, when furniture is arranged, when a restaurant asks for help in deciding where to put tables and booths, or when a store hires a designer to plan the layout of display units— to mention just a few examples.

In every case, the designer must be knowledgeable about building codes and how they affect circulation, requirements for egress, and handicapped accessibility. She must also be aware of standard sizes for furnishings, windows, doors, and human dimensions.

There are a number of methods of approaching space-planning problems. Some of these include matrix charts, bubble diagrams, and block diagrams; adjacency charts and diagrams may be added to this list. Often, several of these techniques are combined in analyzing the space requirements of a particular project.

Space-planning often involves the production of many plans; each plan may be subject to revisions and improvements. Because so many requirements need to be dealt with simultaneously, the act of planning space sometimes resembles that of doing a jigsaw puzzle.

16. Make Space for Our Place: Offices for an Accounting Firm

A CPA firm is moving from one leased space to another. They have asked you to do the space planning for them and have given you a floor plan showing the new space as well as a list of their requirements. They want you to provide them with a plan.

They need the following:

1. *A reception room,* separated from the rest of the office space by a door, which has enough space for four chairs and a small end or coffee table, a 3'-0"-wide coat closet, and the receptionist's desk and equipment. The receptionist's own requirements are: a desk 30" × 60", a typing return 24" × 48", a table 24" × 36" for her computer terminal and printer placed near to her desk, and a small table, perhaps 24" × 24" for the postage meter. In addition, she needs easy access to the firm's copy machine, which can be either in the reception room or in the offices beyond it, but near to the door that separates the two.

2. *A conference room,* which can be without a window, with 1'-0"-deep bookshelves along one wall, which is furnished with a table 4'-0" × 8'-0", six chairs, and a credenza 18" deep × 48" wide.

3. *Partner's office,* with window, approximately 140 square feet. Furnish this office with a desk 36" × 72", an executive chair, two visitors' chairs, and a credenza 18" deep × 72" wide. This partner needs to be near the conference room but does not need to be next to the other partner.

4. *Partner's office,* preferably but not necessarily with window, approximately 120 square feet. Furnish this space with a desk that is 30" × 60" with a 24" × 48" return, an executive chair, and two visitors' chairs.

5. *An open work area* that comfortably accommodates three desks for staff, each 30" × 60" with a 24" × 36" return and six lateral file cabinets, each 18" deep × 36" wide.

6. *A small storage room,* approximately 60 square feet. This space should be interior.

Note: Building code requires a minimum hallway width of 44" and doorways 32" wide. Leave the existing entrance and the windows intact. When you lay out your reception room, be sure you think about the first impression received by clients who walk in the door. You may wish to provide plants and to think about built-in furniture as a possibility for seating in this area. Throughout your space plan, be sure to pay close attention to clearances and circulation patterns.

Further note: Window sill height is 32" and height from finished floor to the acoustical tile ceiling is 8'-0".

PRESENTATION

Floor plan: $\frac{1}{8}$" = 1'-0" scale, showing furniture layout.

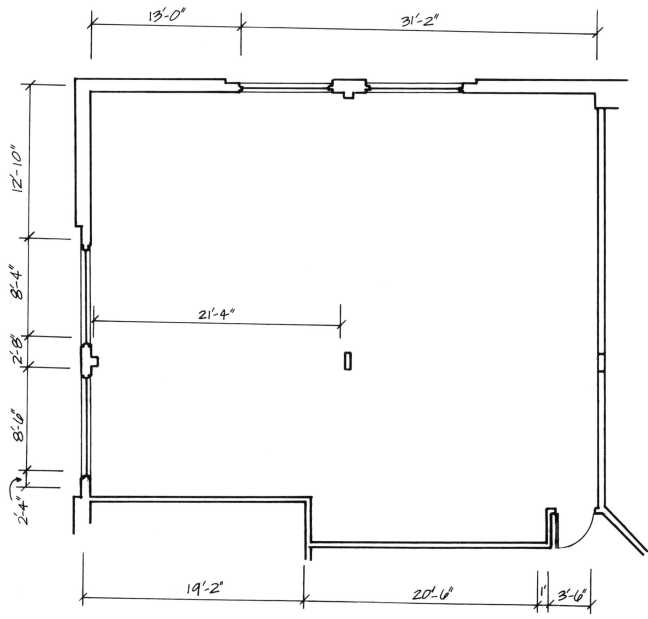

PLAN

Scale: $\frac{1}{8}'' = 1'\text{-}0''$

The accompanying plan shows the configuration of the space that The Charitable Group (fund-raisers for physically challenged children) wants to lease. This group has a "progressive" attitude toward office planning, and they feel that to put the employees into hardwall offices will inhibit communication and efficiency. Therefore, they would like to have you do a layout for them that uses systems furniture, with movable partitions of varying heights. The computer room is the only exception (see below). You will need to think carefully about the heights of the workstation partitions; keep in mind that they need not be uniform.

These are their requirements:

1. *Reception area* with desk for receptionist, seating for four visitors (include a little table), and a coat closet about 4′ wide.

2. *Manager's office* about 150 square feet. The manager needs acoustical privacy, so he will need movable, full-height partitions. His office should be furnished with a standard desk, credenza, executive chair, two visitors' chairs, and a bookcase.

3. *A conference room* to accommodate a table 3′ × 6′ and six chairs. This room, too, requires full-height partitions.

4. *A mailroom* of about 150 square feet, which includes a little counter and a sink. Since the mailroom will require some shelving, it may need to be located on at least one sheetrocked wall. This could be the demising wall (which separates one tenant in the building from another), the wall abutting the hallway, or one of the walls surrounding the computer room. It should not be located on a window wall, however, since windows are best given to offices and workstations.

5. *A computer room* of about 200 square feet. Because this room must be climate-controlled, it will be surrounded by sheetrocked walls.

6. *Workstations* for three administrative assistants, each about 64 square feet.

7. *Workstations* for three assistant managers, each about 120 square feet.

8. *Workstations* for six staff members, each about 100 square feet.

The nine offices for assistant managers and staff will be laid out using systems furniture and movable partitions that are no more

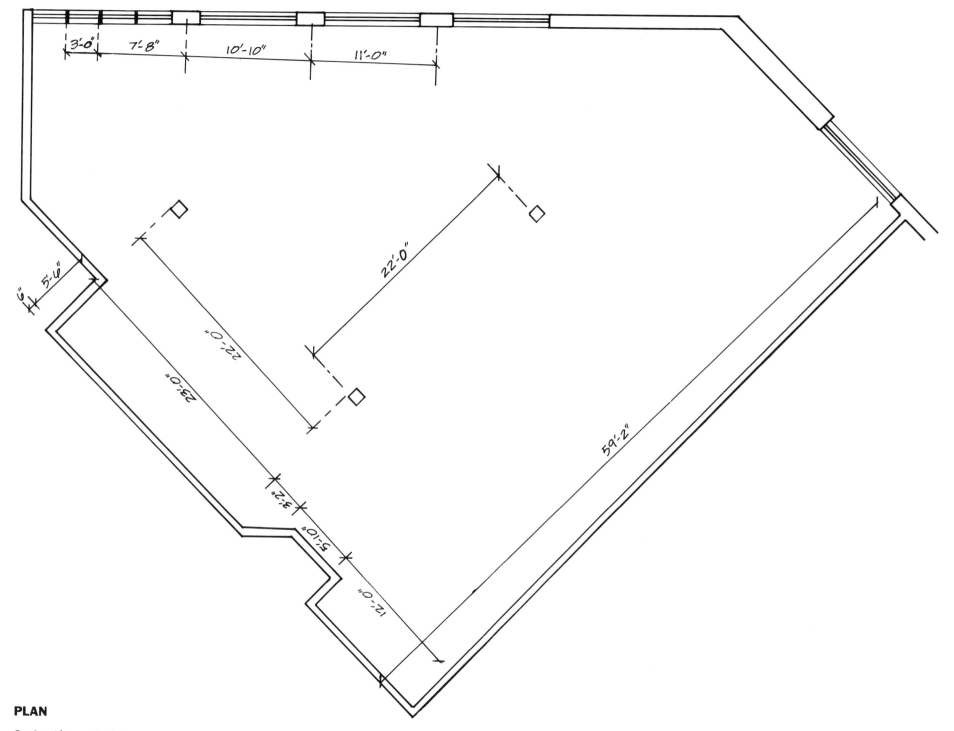

PLAN

Scale: ⅛″ = 1′-0″

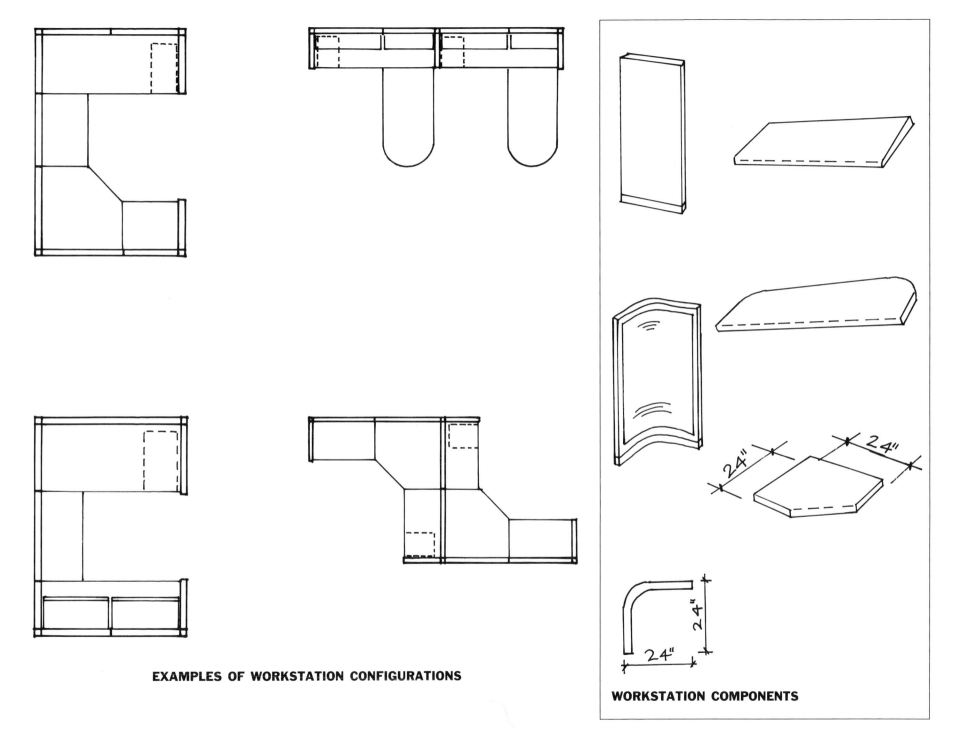

EXAMPLES OF WORKSTATION CONFIGURATIONS

WORKSTATION COMPONENTS

49

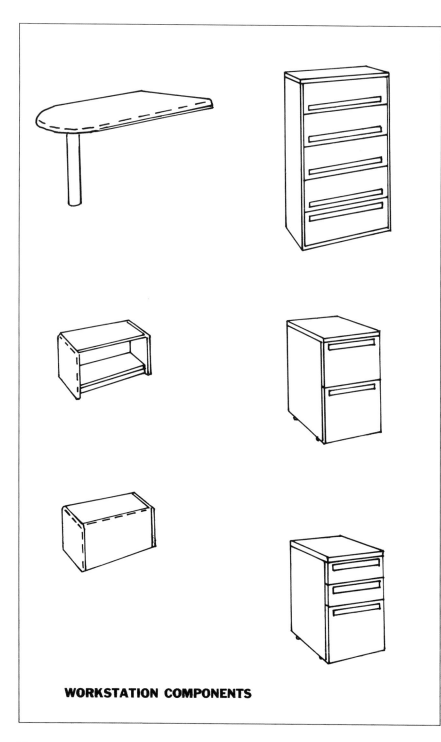

WORKSTATION COMPONENTS

than 5' high. Give each employee workstation an L-shaped work surface configuration, as shown on the illustrations provided, with a place for computer terminal and printer, a 36"-wide × 18"-deep file cabinet, and two visitors' chairs. Use the accompanying illustrations as a guide to the available components from which you can select.

Note: Window sill height is 30". Building code requires that you provide these offices with an emergency exit located as far as possible from the main entrance, that hallway widths be a minimum of 44" wide, and that no dead-end corridors be longer than 20'.

PRESENTATION
Floor plan: ⅛" = 1'-0" scale, showing furniture layout, and with notes necessary to explain partition heights.

Axonometric: This drawing permits you to show how the partition heights you specified affect the overall sense of space within the office.

This project involves planning a small office for a doctor; however, it is slightly complicated by the fact that you will have to determine where to put the office within the available space.

The plan shows the space currently available for lease in a five-story office building. There is no other space in the building. The location is perfect for the doctor, and as the space has been vacant for some time, the owner of the building is eager to lease it. The doctor only wants 600 square feet of space, however. This is less than the available square footage. Both the doctor and the owner are willing to put his office any place within the space shown on the plan, but the owner, who has hired you, asks you to be sure that whatever space is left over will be attractive and easy to lease (probably to another doctor). This means that, as you are planning the doctor's space, you must be sure that you do not give him all the windows or that no awkward, difficult-to-use little spaces are left in the empty area.

The doctor is an endocrinologist who wants to start in private practice. His requirements are fairly simple. He needs a reception area that will seat five and has a place for magazines and a small coat closet. The receptionist is also the secretary. She needs a large work area—big enough for a small computer and a printer, a typewriter, an appointment book, a tabletop copier, and open work surface for writing. In addition, there must be space in her work area for patient files, about 9 linear feet of files, which could be organized in any number of ways—in lateral or vertical file cabinets, or on shelves. The receptionist's work area must be separated from the seating area by a wall. This could be a full-height wall with a glass window or an opening, or a partial-height wall with a transaction counter at the top.

The doctor needs an office for himself, big enough for a desk with return, some bookcases, and two visitors' chairs. His exam room should be no smaller than 10' × 10' and must contain the examination table, a visitor's chair, the doctor's chair, and 5 feet of cabinets (both base and upper) with a small, 18"-stainless steel sink. The exam room and doctor's office should be adjacent, and there should be a pocket, accordion or bifold door in the shared wall, so that the doctor can enter the exam room directly from his office. In some place other than the exam room, you should locate a coffee station. This can be as small as a built-in counter just wide enough for the little undercounter fridge to slide beneath; the coffee pot can sit on the counter.

You will begin this project by quickly trying out different locations for the doctor's office suite. Each time you lay out the space, make a rapid sketch within the leftover space of some imaginary offices for another doctor; this is the way you can be sure that in future, should the owner of the building ask you to plan space for another tenant, the space will in fact be able to be laid out, with rooms of adequate size and access into all the rooms.

Once you have finished your space-planning, you need to give thought to the design of the reception area. Remember that the doctor is just starting out and does not have much money with which to decorate. The finish materials must be low-budget, but attractive. If

you have decided to have a transaction counter built, keep in mind
that many plastic laminates are
now produced in wonderful colors
and patterns and are much cheaper
than wood or stone. On the other
hand, although paint is less expensive than wallcoverings or architectural spray coatings, it is much
more difficult to keep clean and
maintain; in this instance, it makes
more sense to spend a bit more on
materials that will last longer and
look nicer. Can you find some seats
that are economical but do not look
like those in every doctor's waiting
room you've ever seen?

Note: The window sill height is
32″, and the height from floor to
suspended ceiling is 8′-0″. Building code requires hallways that are
a minimum of 44″ wide. No emergency exit is needed for tenant
areas of less than 2,000 square feet.

PRESENTATION

Floor plan: ¼″ = 1′-0″ scale,
showing placement of all furniture
and equipment. The floor plan
should show the entire plan, with
both the doctor's office and the adjacent space. The leftover area
should be laid out with a reception
area, and as many offices and exam
rooms as can reasonably fit. The requirements for this space would be
similiar to those you have planned
in detail. The endocrinologist's of-

fices should be rendered in color,
but the adjacent area should be labeled, not rendered, and shown
with no furniture. The sole purpose of showing this secondary
plan is to demonstrate that you
have made a sensible decision in
determining the location of the
doctor's space.

Perspective of waiting room, showing finish materials, furniture, and
other details, rendered.

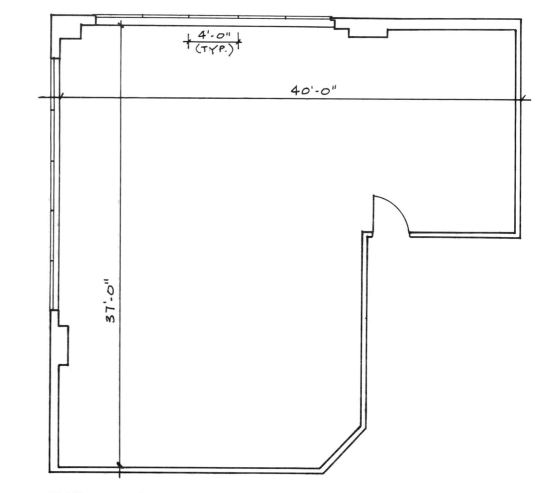

PLAN Scale: ⅛″ = 1′-0″

After months of searching for just the right office building in which to locate the offices of her newly established magazine publication business, Jane Doe feels she has succeeded. The owner of the building has given her a drawing of the available space and asked her to return as soon as possible with a plan showing the buildout. Jane sat down to make some sketches but quickly found herself unable to figure out where to put the main entrance! She has called and asked you to do a couple of space plans to help her in making the decision.

The accompanying plan shows the space, shaped like an L. It is on the second story of the building, and the interior glass wall overlooks the lobby on the first floor, with its granite floor and collection of plants. Jane feels it would be nice to locate the reception area or conference room on this interior glass wall, but she does not want to plan it this way unless it functions well within the total scheme. She also feels it might be nice to locate her salespeople, who are in cubicles with movable partitions, along this wall. She would like you to come up with two different plans. In one, the main entry would be located near the interior glass wall, with the reception or conference rooms located along that wall. In the other, the main entry could be anywhere, and the salespeople would be located along the interior glass wall.

These are Jane's overall requirements:

1. *Reception area* to accommodate a receptionist in an $8' \times 8'$ workstation, seating for four people (four chairs and a table or two), and a small coat closet. In or near this area you must provide a similarly sized workstation for a secretary.
2. *A copy machine,* fax machine, and three 36"-wide lateral file cabinets located close to the receptionist.
3. *A conference room* suitable for seating eight people.
4. *Five private offices,* approximately the same size (about $12' \times 12'$). In each office, provide a desk with return, a chair, two visitors' chairs, and a small bookcase. The people who will occupy these offices are: Jane Doe, president; John Doe, vice president (her son); Mandy Miller (editor); Lottie (assistant to the editor); and Radha (sales manager). The president's and vice president's offices should be adjacent to one another. They would also like to be near the conference room. Ideally, the conference room would also be placed not too far from the reception area, but this is less critical.
5. *Workstations* for six salespeople, each $6' \times 6'$. Provide each with as much work surface as possible, including a corner keyboard unit, an overcounter storage bin, and pedestals with drawers. Radha's office should be near those of the salespeople, whom she oversees.
6. *An additional seven lateral files* near the workstations, each 36" wide.
7. *A mini-kitchen,* wherever you can. This should consist of no more than 6' of cabinets, a small sink, and an undercounter fridge.

Note: This office space will also require an emergency exit, located as far as is feasible from the main entry. Building code requires that the exit be accessible from a hallway no less than 44" wide that is not blocked by doors or furniture. Another code requirement states that no subsidiary dead end hallway (leading off the principal hallway) may be longer than $20'$-$0"$ long.

PRESENTATION
Two floor plans, as described above, in $\frac{1}{8}" = 1'$-$0"$ scale.

As a part of your final presentation, explain which of the two plans you think works best from the point of view of adjacencies, circulation patterns, and employee satisfaction.

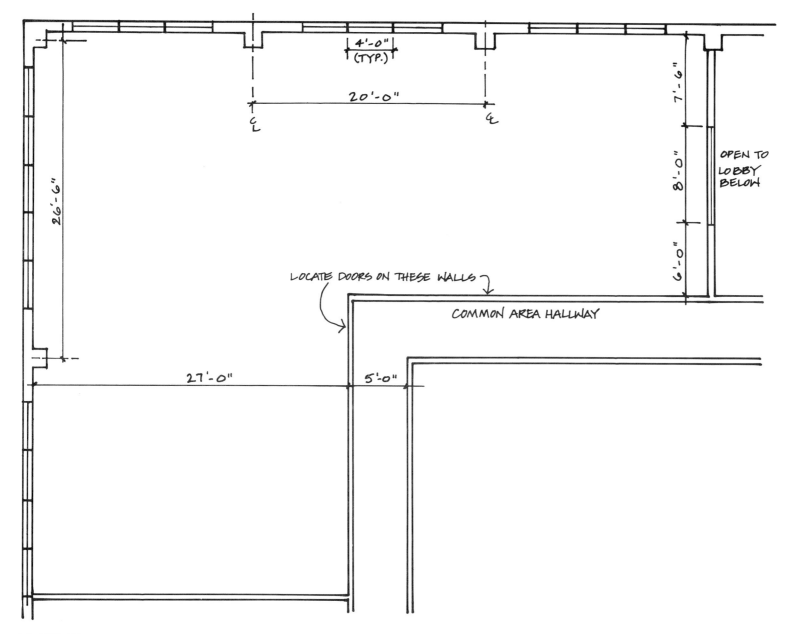

4'-0"
(TYP.)

20'-0"

7'-6"

8'-0"

OPEN TO
LOBBY
BELOW

6'-0"

26'-6"

LOCATE DOORS ON THESE WALLS

COMMON AREA HALLWAY

27'-0"

5'-0"

FLOOR PLAN

Scale: ⅛″ = **1′-0**″

20. Develop Plans for a Developer

It often happens that when the owner/developer of a new office building takes prospective tenants through the space, he or she finds that they have trouble visualizing their offices built out. The space they are looking at is raw: concrete floors, structural columns, and exposed ducts and electrical work. They have difficulty with the mental transformation of this space into reception and conference rooms and carpeted offices, particularly if the space is in any way unusual in its configuration or if their needs are complicated.

Owners or their agents will sometimes hire space-planners, designers, or architects to create hypothetical office suites on an office floor, so that they can show potential tenants what their offices *might* look like. Although the plans produced do not show the offices of a real client, they do demonstrate how firms of different sizes, with fairly standard requirements, would lay out in the building. This is often helpful to the owner of the building, too.

For this project, you are given the floor plan, drawn at $1/16'' = 1'-0''$ scale, of an office building. You

will first need to draw the plan to $1/8'' = 1'-0''$ scale, using your scale and the given dimensions. Your goal in this project is to subdivide the floor into several office suites of *varying* sizes. In so doing, you will help the owner of the building to see how best to break up the floor. Some typical tenant sizes might be: 1,000 square feet, 1,500 square feet, 2,000 square feet, and so on. Thus, you might decide to lay out several small tenant spaces of 1,500 or 2,000 square feet and one or two larger tenant spaces.

For each space, you will show a "typical" office layout. This could include a reception area with seating and a closet, a conference room, perhaps a storage room, perhaps a coffee station or tiny kitchenette, an equipment room for fax, copier, mail machine and such, private offices, and maybe open workstations for secretarial support. You might decide to design offices for a business with different requirements, such as one that provides classes in a training or demo room. One way for you to find out what kinds of rooms and spaces are needed by typical businesses is to interview some owners or managers.

The process of dividing up the floor into suites and of laying out rooms within those suites may or may not take place simultaneously. You can carve out the larger chunks first, then plan the individual rooms, or you can do both at once; you may find that the design of a particular group of offices will affect the size and configuration of the office group adjacent to it. Be sure to label all spaces (e.g. Reception, Administrative Assistant ($8' \times 8'$), File Room, etc.). You should always label the office suite with the name of the business: e.g., Romano Travel Agency, Harcutt and Blowdri, Attorneys-at-Law, and so on. Complete your drawing by showing all the furniture and plants and the pattern of flooring material.

Finally, you will determine and draw the finishes and furniture, if any, in the lobby. The color of walls, of course, will not show on a plan, but any pattern of tile or carpet, in addition to the placement of furniture and plants, will be seen.

You may invent a title block for this drawing, and it might read something like: Typical Multiten-

ant Office Layout for the Braun Building. Remember to note your $1/8'' = 1'-0''$ scale. Often drawings like these are mounted in the lobbies of such buildings or are shown to potential tenants during a presentation by an owner or commercial real estate broker.

PRESENTATION

Entire floor plan, subdivided into tenant spaces with rooms labeled, furniture shown, floor patterns indicated, colored, and mounted on a board.

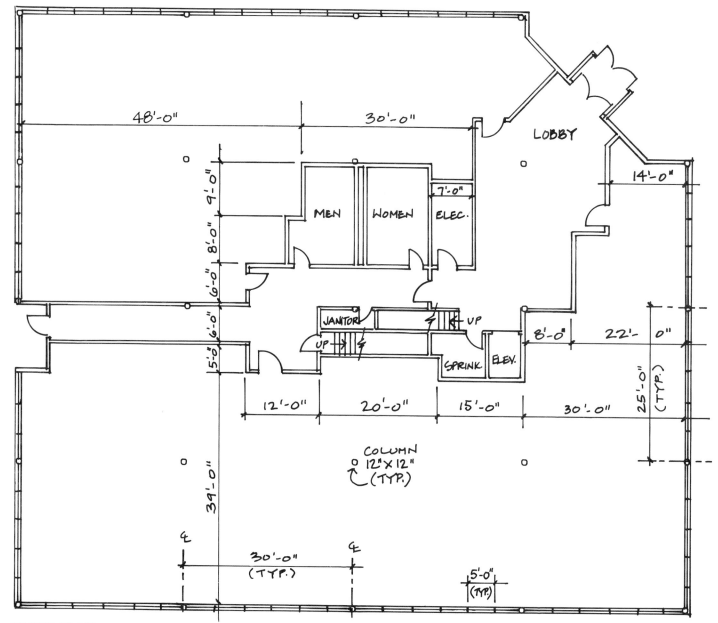

48'-0"   30'-0"

LOBBY

14'-0"

9'-0"

7'-0"

MEN   WOMEN   ELEC.

8'-0"

6'-0"

5'-0"

JANITOR   UP

UP   SPRINK   ELEV.

8'-0"   22'-0"

25'-0"
(TYP.)

12'-0"   20'-0"   15'-0"   30'-0"

COLUMN
12"×12"
(TYP.)

39'-0"

30'-0"
(TYP.)

5'-0"
(TYP.)

FLOOR PLAN

Scale: $\frac{1}{16}'' = 1'\text{-}0''$

Section V

Selection of Furniture and Finish Materials

PROJECTS

The projects in this section encourage you to explore the effects of changes in furniture style as well as finishes such as carpet and wallcovering, and ceiling and lighting design. Projects include both residential and commercial spaces and vary in scope.

The subject is vast. Within the context of residential design alone, you can study the history of furniture and become knowledgeable about styles both antique and modern; you can think about the differences between movable and built-in furniture; you can also learn to design custom-built furniture for those situations in which you cannot find exactly the right item. For commercial interiors, you will need to become familiar with the different manufacturers of both freestanding and systems furniture for offices, as well as for hotel and restaurant spaces. In the case of retail interiors, you will learn that designers frequently create custom display units.

Your choice of furniture will be determined by a number of different considerations. You must think about the uses to which the furniture will be put. For example, if you are making selections for a living room, you need to know how that space will be used. Is it a room in which guests are entertained but not used otherwise? If so, you may

feel that you can safely specify delicate upholstery fabrics such as silk. You may want to incorporate antiques that would not withstand rough treatment from children. Are community meetings held there? In this case, smaller furniture that can be clustered in a variety of ways may be more appropriate. Does it include a television set or stereo system? Does its owner need to provide for the display of special artworks? The answers to all these and other questions will help to determine your approach.

You will also select furniture on the basis of its design. Choices include antiques (both genuine and reproduction), contemporary, postmodern, or handcrafted. Each of these types has distinct characteristics and associations. We tend to think of period furniture as formal and elaborate, and of contemporary pieces as more casual. "Modern" furniture, which actually refers to those pieces exemplified by the Bauhaus movement of the 1920s and 1930s, is simple, functional, and often emphasizes high-tech materials. The classic Breuer chair, with which you are probably familiar, is an example.

When you specify furniture for an interior, you have to assess its comfort, construction, and materials;

all of these must be appropriate to the use to which the furniture is put. Whether the piece in question is of wood or is upholstered, color and pattern will be considerations.

At the same time that you are designing your space and selecting your furniture, you will have to choose finish materials. Once again, the choices are many. The floor may be covered with wood (which can be natural in color or stained), carpet, rugs, vinyl tile, marble, or ceramic tiles. The walls may be painted (with one or many colors), sprayed with an architectural coating (particularly in commercial settings), or covered with paper, grasscloth, cork, or vinyl wallcovering, to name just a few. The ceiling can also be made of a number of different materials. In a residence, sheetrock is probably most commonly used, but in commercial interiors one sees a variety of acoustical tiles, metal, and wood.

Your selection of furniture styles and finish materials will affect the emotional response of the user. In the introduction to Section II, "Manipulating Space," you learned that you can influence the way in which the user experiences the space through your design decisions. This is also true with respect to furniture and finish choices. You can create interiors that are excit-

ing or soothing, surprising or familiar, casual or formal. Your choices can be traditional or avant-garde. Furniture (including artwork and decorative accessories) and finishes are another part of your design vocabulary.

21. Different Looks for Different Cooks: A Kitchen Renovation

Using the two perspectives provided, which give you two views of the same kitchen, select cabinets, appliances, finishes, and colors to meet the needs of two different clients.

Your first client is Babette, a French actress who has bought a condominium in Los Angeles to use whenever she films in the United States. The kitchen is small, but she is willing to spend a good deal of money to make it very nice. The look she wants is French country, with rustic surfaces, decorated tiles, and natural materials. She likes to read while eating at the center island; she will need a comfortable stool and a pendant lamp above the island. Over time she has collected some attractive pots, ceramic canisters, and utensils, and she would like to display these in the kitchen. She wants a homey, cozy atmosphere.

Your second client is Anya, who lives in San Francisco but has purchased a beautiful vacation house on the Northern California coast. The house is not large, but it is spectacular, with long expanses of glass overlooking the ocean. It is furnished simply, with Shaker-style furniture, white area rugs on polished wooden floors, and dramatic artworks. Its kitchen is small, but she does not plan to enlarge it. Rather, she would like you to select cabinets and finishes that make the space appear large and airy. She prefers a sleek, contemporary look; she loves high-gloss Italian cabinetry in bright colors as well as white or light-colored wood cabinets. She likes appliances which can be faced with panels to match the cabinets, which gives the whole kitchen a very built-in look; she also likes to keep all the surfaces uncluttered.

PRESENTATION

Develop two perspectives for each client, using the outlines provided, but filling in the details, including: cabinets, appliances, window design and treatment, finish materials, accessories, and lighting. You may draw in things like cookbooks, utensils, plants, or other objects to give life to the drawing. The drawings should be colored.

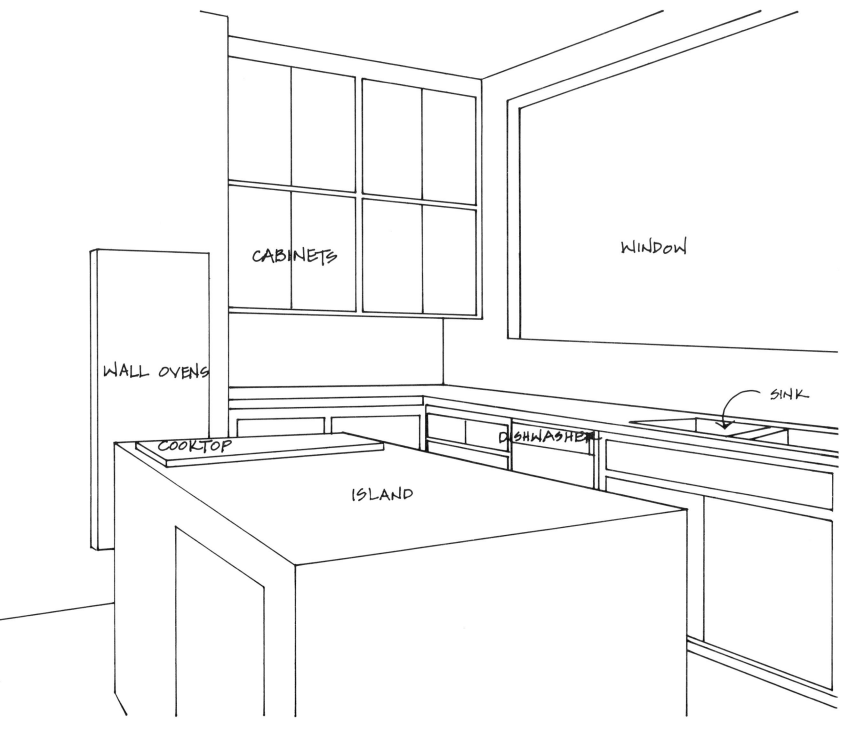

WALL OVENS

CABINETS

WINDOW

SINK

COOKTOP

DISHWASHER

ISLAND

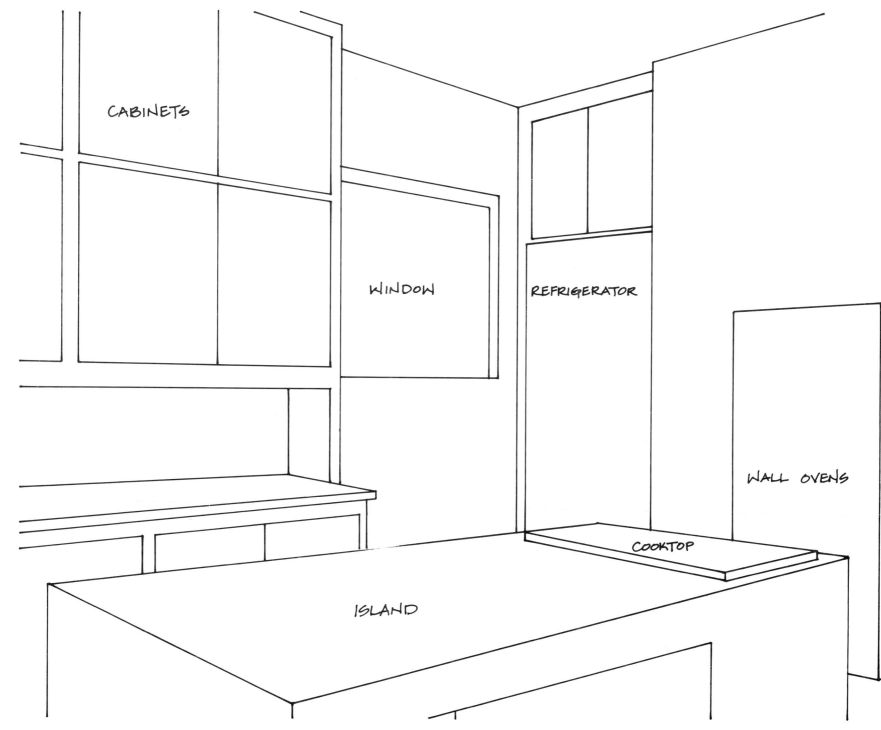

CABINETS

WINDOW

REFRIGERATOR

WALL OVENS

COOKTOP

ISLAND

PERSPECTIVE

22. Lobby Redo: An Uncommon Common Area

The perspective view and plan show the existing interior of the lobby of a small office building in suburban New York. The building is half empty and its office space has been difficult to lease. It has recently been sold to a new owner, who wishes to update and improve the lobby decor, in order to make the building more attractive and therefore easier to rent. You have been hired to make new finish selections, as well as to create a seating area and to decorate the space with plants and artwork—in short, to make a beautiful new space that will appeal to the corporate executives who will be working in the building.

In preparation for this project, it would be useful for you to visit any small office buildings in your area to see how their lobby interiors are handled; you will see lots of poorly done interiors that you will not want to imitate! You should also look through the trade magazines for pictures of lobby interiors; these will often be too elaborate. You need to select furniture and finishes that are not too grand, as this is not a major downtown building but a small suburban one. At the same time, your design so-lution should be carefully considered; you do not want to make the most predictable and common-place choices.

PRESENTATION

Enlarge the ⅛″ = 1′-0″ scale plan to ¼″ scale. A perspective outline is provided, if you wish to use it, and you may extend and enlarge it. Produce a floor plan and two perspectives, rendered in color, that fully demonstrate your intentions and make your design approach clear. Next to the floor plan you should show a finish and furniture schedule and next to or below the perspective, you should attach samples of your finish materials and careful drawings of your furniture selections.

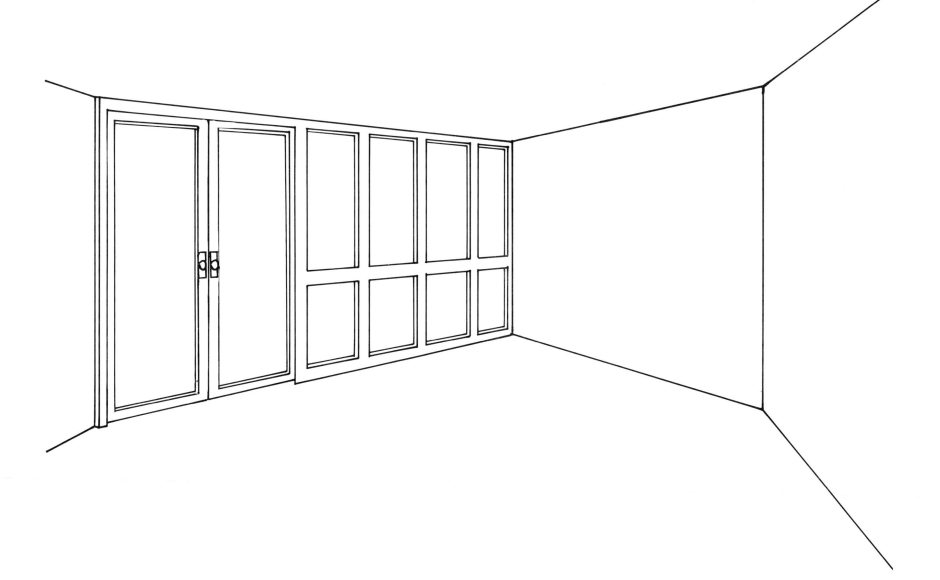

PERSPECTIVE

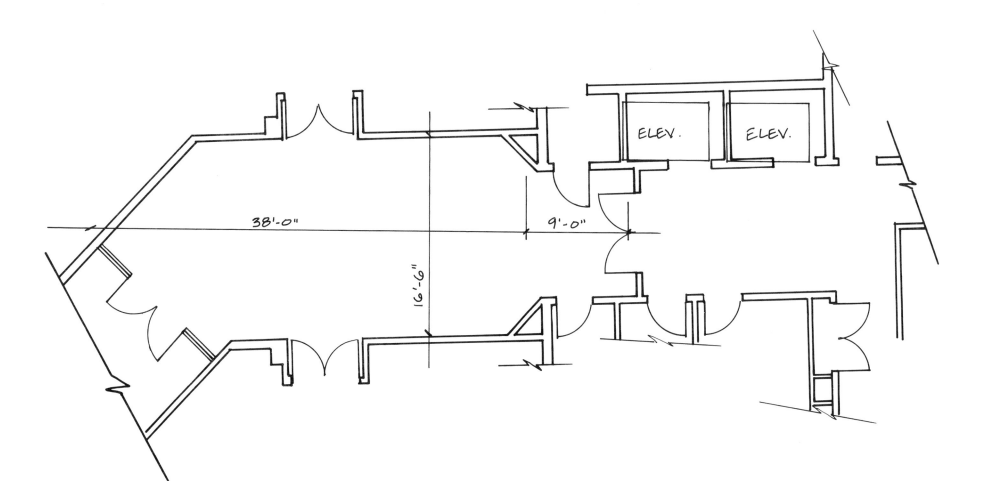

PLAN

Scale: ⅛″ = **1′-0″**

23. A Showroom for Surfaces: A Dramatic Reception Area

In the room shown by the plan, you are to create a very dramatic reception area for Surfaces, Inc. This company, which markets plastic laminates, will be adding a new line: exciting new plastic laminates designed and produced in Asia. The new products have a wide color range as well as unusual patterns that are contemporary and even avant-garde. The look is new and "now."

Surfaces leases interior space in a Design Center, and they plan a grand opening to introduce the new products to architects and designers. Their total space includes a large conference/showroom (which they are leaving in its existing condition) and a smaller reception area, which they wish you to redesign, emphasizing the new product. Since this is the space seen upon first entering, the Surfaces partners are eager to make a powerful first impression.

You should include areas for comfortable seating and for the receptionist's station. The receptionist needs a station about $10' \times 10'$, with counter big enough for a telephone, computer, and printer. The seating area should accommodate six people and include at least one table.

The emphasis in this project should be on the display of the product. Find as many imaginative and attractive ways as possible to showcase the new laminates. One obvious approach is to design the receptionist's station—perhaps including a transaction counter and a dropped soffit—with a veneer of one or several laminate colors. You should, however, develop some other ideas, whether functional, decorative, or both. (You might, for example, frame pieces of laminate and hang them as though they are pictures. You might design custom seating that incorporates laminate surfaces.)

PRESENTATION
Model: $\frac{1}{2}'' = 1'-0''$ scale. You can build the model of foam-core board and use any of several materials to indicate color, including Color-Aid paper, wallpaper, drawings you have made on plain paper, or anything else you can think of. These materials may be used to represent the laminate surfaces as well as others. The model's roof should be removable and the door openings shown, so that the initial view through the entrance into the room may be seen.

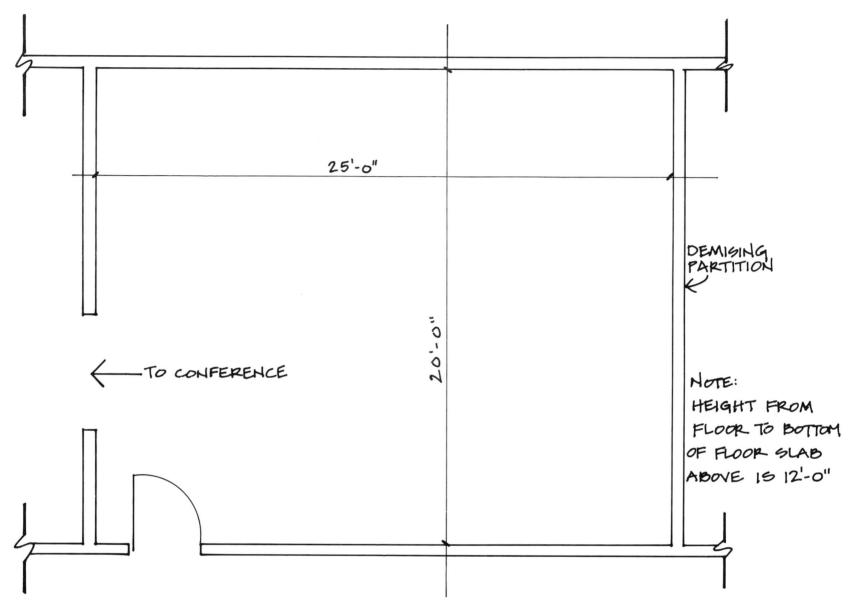

25'-0"

DEMISING
PARTITION

TO CONFERENCE

20'-0"

NOTE:
HEIGHT FROM
FLOOR TO BOTTOM
OF FLOOR SLAB
ABOVE IS 12'-0"

PLAN

Scale: ¼″ = 1′-0″

The space-planning and furniture layout for Estelle's restaurant are done for you (see plans). Your job, as interior designer, is to make architectural detail, finish material, furniture, and accessory selections that will successfully create the ambience Estelle desires. You need to think, in other words, about both specific detail and general atmosphere.

Note: The stairs labeled "down" go to the basement, whereas those labeled "up" lead to apartments on the second level. Place the two plans together in such a way that the stairs overlap, in order to obtain a picture of the entire first floor.

You will consider the following:

Flooring: Hard surface (like wood or tile) or soft (carpet), or a combination; think about flooring pattern and how it might relate to circulation patterns, ceiling design, or other finish patterns.
Walls: Finish (paint, vinyl wall-covering, fabric, spray-applied architectural coating, or a combination), texture, and color.
Ceiling: Drywall, acoustical tile, wood, metal, or a combination;

one level or more.
Lighting: Direct, indirect, or both; fluorescent, incandescent, halogen, neon.
Architectural detailing: Casings, moldings, baseboards, casework, custom built-ins, styles of windows and door.
Furniture: Custom-built breakfast counter (see plan), stools and chairs, tables; the tables, stools, and chairs may be either stock or custom.
Accessories: Artwork, plants, window treatment.

Remember that you may wish to make specifications that are non-standard—for example, to spray an architectural coating onto surfaces other than walls (like doors or furniture). You should feel free in this project to be as creative as you can; restaurants, like store interiors, may be very distinctive.

SCENARIO #1: ESTELLE'S: A COUNTRY PLACE IN THE CITY

Estelle has just moved to a large southern city and has purchased an antebellum house in an attractive part of town that she plans to convert into an inn. The house is built in a traditional southern style, with two-story columns and a large

veranda. Upstairs, the house will have bedrooms and suites available for rent. Estelle will convert the first floor into a restaurant, reception area, and small gift shop, which will serve not only the guests at the inn but also the general public.

The food is American nouvelle cuisine: pasta, quiche, special soups, and spectacular baked goods. The atmosphere should be elegant but quiet, a mixture of New England country inn and southern hospitality. Estelle likes flowers, antiques, and high-quality materials. However, she is asking you, her designer, to create an interior style that appeals to her but is neither completely traditional nor predictable; she wants Estelle's place to convey an image that, though elegant and with wide appeal, is nevertheless unique.

SCENARIO #2: ESTELLE'S: NOT QUITE SOUTH OF THE BORDER

Estelle has moved to the outskirts of a large southwestern city, where she has bought an old Spanish Colonial house, in which she will open a Mexican restaurant. The food will not be Mexican fast food, but unusual regional dishes from different parts of Mexico. Therefore, although the building is traditional, the menu is not, and Estelle does not want a typical Mexican interior. Rather, she wants you to use the various elements of Mexican art and architecture—and your imagination—to come up with an approach that has a south-of-the-border atmosphere, but that is really different and, above all, fun!

She expects her clients to be young urban professionals coming from the city. They already have access to many sophisticated and interesting restaurants in the city and will not travel to Estelle's unless her cuisine and decor are truly special.

You should think about traditional and contemporary Mexican architecture, textures, materials, colors, about Mexican folk crafts, the Mexican landscape, and its history (great Indian civilizations, like the Maya and Aztec, as well as the Spanish colonial period). From all these elements, you will develop an exciting interior for your client, Estelle.

PRESENTATION

For each scenario, you will produce a rendered floor plan, a detailed perspective, and a materials board.

Floor plan: Scale: ¼" = 1'-0". The accompanying plan(s) show the furniture layout. You will leave the general furniture layout and space plan intact, as well as the location of door and windows. You may, however, wish to change the shape of tables, chairs, or counter. You will also show on your plan: flooring material and pattern and any added elements such as new partitions, plants, columns, and so on.

Perspective: The purpose of the perspective is to give a full and realistic view of all your design decisions, including the furniture selections, the wall and window treatments, counter design, accessories, artwork, and so on. Do not forget to show ceiling and lighting design! Therefore, choose a point of view that most fully reveals the interior space and make your perspective as complete as possible. (For the purpose of constructing the perspective, assume a ceiling height of 9'-1".)

Materials board: On the board, mount and label all the finishes you are selecting for the restaurant; you may also wish to show neat drawings of furniture not viewed in your perspective.

Floor plan and perspective should be rendered in color.

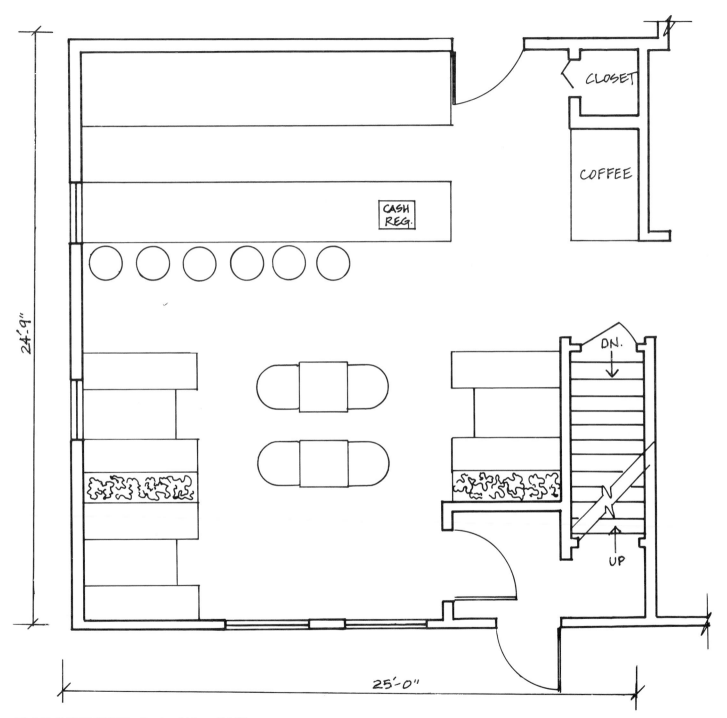

CLOSET

COFFEE

CASH REG.

DN.

UP

24'-9"

25'-0"

PLAN (LEFT SIDE) Scale: ¼" = 1'-0"

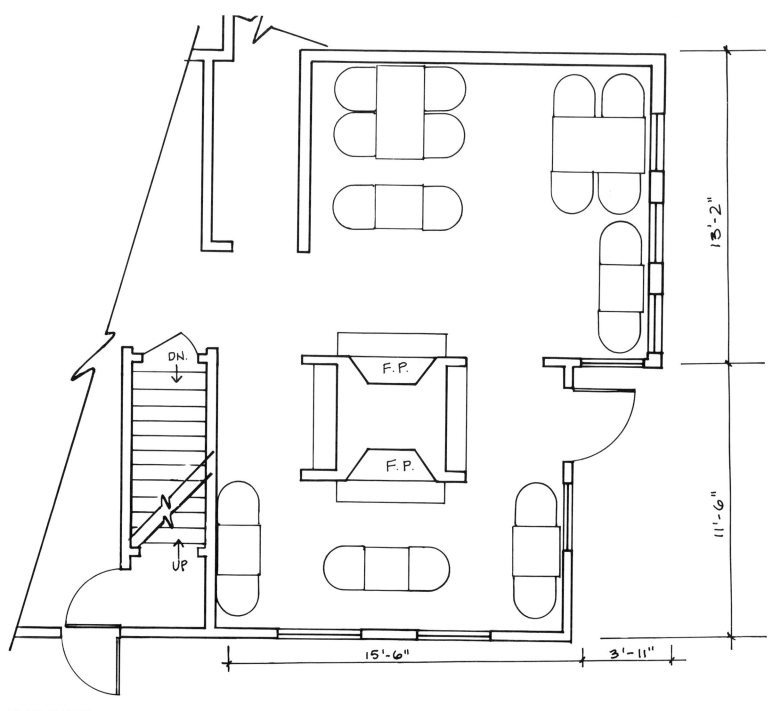

13'-2"

11'-6"

DN.

UP

F.P.

F.P.

15'-6"

3'-11"

PLAN (RIGHT SIDE) Scale: ¼" = 1'-0"

Note to the instructor: this project proposes six different scenarios, so that you can select from a wide variety, choosing as many as you feel appropriate for your class.

For this project, you will choose furniture, decorative objects, finish materials, and lighting for an interior shown in a very simplified form in the following schematic perspective drawing. Certain aspects of the interior are given and should not be changed; these are the architectural features such as the fireplace, windows, door, ceiling height, and the furniture layout.

Working within these constraints, your job as designer is to make the appropriate selections for your clients. One purpose of this exercise is to help you to become familiar with the large variety of existing materials and resources for interior designers. Another is to give you practice in making choices that create an environment and an atmosphere that express the character of a specific client. Use your architectural scale to determine furniture sizes, which may be considered approximate. Keep in mind that the furniture shown in

the perspective is drawn to show you location and scale, to help you in making sketches for the interiors you design, and is in no way intended to look like specific items. You should draw a plan and a perspective that show the style of furniture, floor pattern, wall and window treatments, and colors you have chosen.

Study the drawings and, for each client, consider the following:

1. *Flooring material(s) and pattern:* Choices include tile (marble, granite, vinyl, ceramic), carpet, sheet vinyl flooring, and wood.
2. *Wallcovering(s):* Choices include paint, wallpaper, and spray-applied architectural coatings.
3. *Window treatment(s):* Choices include a wide variety of curtains, shades, and horizontal or vertical blinds.
4. *Furniture:* Think about style (traditional, contemporary, avant-garde, antique, and custom), fixed and movable, materials (painted or unpainted wood, plastic, metal), and fabric (color, fiber, and pattern).
5. *Lighting:* Choices include ambient and task, fluorescent, incandescent, and halogen.

6. *Accessories and artwork:* Think about art for walls (paintings, prints, posters, tapestries), sculptural objects, crafts, plants, flowers, mirrors, antiques, folk art, etc.

A CONDOMINIUM

The drawings show the interior of part of a waterfront condominium in a large northeastern city such as Boston. From the deck, one can see the marina and part of the downtown area. During the day, the sun sparkles on the water and on the reflective glass surfaces of the skyscrapers; at night, the lights from offices and cars streaming along the waterfront highway are dazzling.

The condo is on the fifteenth floor of its building; its windows overlook a small park.

This part of the condo is the living/dining area. It is furnished with a sofa, console and coffee tables, two chairs, dining table with chairs, and cabinetry along one wall, which houses a TV, a VCR, stereo, books, and accessories. The doorway leads into an entrance hall that separates this room from the kitchen.

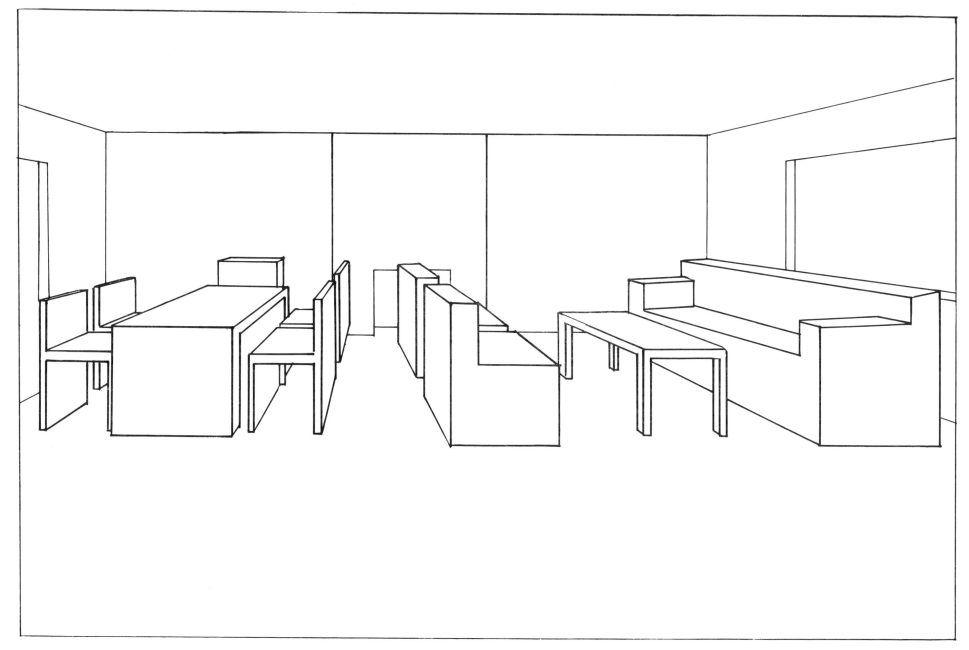

PERSPECTIVE OUTLINE

The client is Ray, a successful thirty-one-year-old financial analyst who works in nearby downtown. Ray leads and loves the single life. He travels often, has many friends, and likes to entertain in his condo. He also likes to relax by going to the theatre and reading. He is not a serious collector, but he does enjoy primitive and folk art, and he has bought a few nice pieces on his travels to Mexico and Southeast Asia that he wants to feature in this room.

A CONFERENCE ROOM

The drawings show the conference room of a partner in a large urban law firm. The firm has three dozen partners and a varied practice. The offices occupy four floors of a ten-story building in the heart of downtown. The sliding doors open onto a balcony that overlooks a busy street; thus, the balcony is not really used much.

The lawyer is Paula. Her practice concerns divorce and child custody, so she uses this conference room to meet with individual clients and with small family groups. The doorway leads into her office.

Paula wants this room to reflect the character of the firm, which is successful and has an established reputation. The interior should also be a comfortable and comforting place for distressed clients to unburden themselves to their lawyer. It is a place where Paula sometimes sits and reads or prepares a case. Finally, it is also a small, in-house conference room, where Paula meets with her colleagues. It is furnished with two kinds of meeting areas: a table with chairs and soft seating. Along the wall are shelves containing Paula's books.

A WAITING ROOM

The drawings show the waiting room of a small, suburban pediatric practice. This office is located on a moderately busy street that is zoned commercial and multifamily; the building was at one time a large, nineteenth-century single family residence in the style known as Greek Revival. The doorway leads to an adjacent space with the receptionist and the coat closet; this room was probably at one time a large parlor. The floor is the original oak, the walls plaster, and there is some decorative plaster molding in good condition. The sliding doors are a later addition; they open onto a contemporary deck that abuts a pleasant, treed backyard.

Because this is a pediatric office, the furniture, materials, and colors should be appropriate for use by children as well as the adults who accompany them; for instance, the table and chairs could be scaled to suit children, and the shelving might be storage for toys and childrens' books. Furniture should be safe for use by children, unlikely to tip or break and with no sharp corners. Materials should probably be pretty durable, although this is not a high-traffic interior.

In addition, the doctors want to preserve the nineteenth-century character of the room as much as possible, so your task as designer is to combine aspects of an antique residence with those of a contemporary commercial space and to make this combination work well.

A SHOWROOM FOR
MEMPHIS FURNITURE

The drawings show a small room that is one of several making up a showroom for the line of Italian furniture known as Memphis. This collection, established in the early 1980s by Italian architect Ettore Sottsass, is known for odd and unexpected shapes and materials. The aim of the designers was to break with the Modern tradition of sleek and streamlined, neutral-colored furniture. Thus, the Memphis pieces are wildly colored, highly patterned, and individualistic. Inexpensive materials such as plastic laminate and expensive materials like marble are sometimes used together in a piece of furniture.

The showroom is located on the first floor of an old armory building in San Francisco that has been converted to a Design Center open to the trade only. The doorway leads into a larger room similarly laid out with Memphis pieces, while the sliding glass doors, installed at some earlier time before the building was converted to its present use, are kept permanently locked. The view is of San Francisco's Embarcadero. Your clients are the owners of the showroom, and your job as designer is to select a few Memphis pieces for the showroom and to choose finishes and accessories that best enhance the furniture pieces, keeping in mind that this is a retail operation.

A TEACHERS' LOUNGE

The drawings show part of the teachers' break room and lounge in a public high school located in a suburb of a large midwestern city. The sliding glass doors lead to a courtyard ringed by the one-story school building. The courtyard is not a play area but has some picnic benches at which students eat lunch in good weather and is landscaped with some trees and grassy areas. The doorway of the lounge leads into a large room with kitchen and some additional tables. The cabinetry along the long wall may be designed to accommodate storage units for individual

teachers (like lockers) as well as food storage.

The school is undergoing renovation, and you are a member of the design team awarded the job; you have been asked to improve this space. Currently, the walls are tan, the floor is a dull brown vinyl tile, and the furniture is a collection of mismatched chrome, plastic, and laminate items that are in a bad state of repair and need replacement. Your budget is limited, so you will need to choose finishes and furniture reasonable in cost as well as durable. The teachers are looking forward to a new look, both relaxing and cheerful.

LIBRARY READING ROOM

The drawings show a small adult reading room in the branch library of a medium-sized southwestern city, furnished with soft seating, table and chairs, and magazine display shelves along one wall. The sliders lead into a pleasant, enclosed courtyard with sand-colored brick paths, benches and a large, landscaped area in its center with palms, cacti, and other native plants. The doorway leads to a corridor and to the card catalog. This space is always very quiet; it is not intended to provide general access to the courtyard.

The library staff has asked you to make your selections appropriate to

the southwestern location, which means that colors, patterns, artwork, and so on will need to have a southwestern flavor. In addition, they want the room to be quite subdued and not overdecorated, as it must function as a space in which people can read and concentrate.

PRESENTATION

For each client, show:

Floor plan: ¼" = 1'-0" scale minimum, with furniture layout, in color.

Perspective: Detailed drawing, in color.

Materials and furniture selections on a separate board.

Section VI
Human Factors

PROJECTS

An interior designer, it has been said, must consider not only aesthetic but functional issues when working on a project. It has also been emphasized that the designer must listen carefully to the client, produce a complete program, and create an interior that meets the clients' needs. These needs could include wheelchair accessibility, acoustical control, adequate ventilation, comfortable seating at a computer terminal, good lighting —in fact, all the concerns that affect user comfort and satisfaction.

Although designers give lip service to the notion that client needs must be met, the fact is that many buildings have been created that, although beautiful, do not function well. One example involves the construction of a five-story office building in Canada. The building was designed with a five-story atrium in the center, overlooked by each of the five floors. In addition, each floor was designed with an open plan, using low partitions, so that every part of the building was open to the others. After the building had been occupied for a short while, it became evident that, with no walls to inhibit the noise of conversations or of typewriters and other equipment, employees could not concentrate. The solution was to retrofit the building with white noise (the sound made by a fan) that covered up other sounds. Un-

fortunately, this was expensive. If the designers had taken the ambient noise level into consideration when planning the space, they might have found another way to solve the problem that was cheaper and more efficient.

All designers should, of course, be sensitive to the issues of the kind mentioned above. In actual practice, some designers remain largely unaware of the importance of human factors in design. Others confront it directly in the design of interiors for such specialized populations as nursing home residents, hospital or hospice patients, residents in low-income housing projects or shelters for the homeless, children in day care centers, and so on.

Partly as a result of user dissatisfaction, the study of human factors has developed. The term "human factors" is a comprehensive one that includes a number of specialized areas of concern. Among these are: ergonomics (the relationship of human dimensions to design, particularly in the design of office furnishings), barrier-free design, design for children, user safety and security, psychology, and environmental considerations, among others. The questions raised by a study of human factors in design are absolutely fundamental. They have to do with peoples' attitudes toward

one another, their needs for privacy as well as social interaction, their desire for social ranking, their territorial behavior, and their responses to crowding. (Many very interesting books and articles have been written on this subject, which can only be touched upon here.)

It is important for you to understand, too, that the environments in which people live consist not simply of rooms or buildings but of villages, towns, and cities, with or without green space. Thus, you are designing interior space within a larger context of which you must always remain aware.

A group of neurologists have asked you to help them design their new offices; they have outgrown their existing space. They know you have a good eye for finishes and furniture and that you are a good space-planner. They are choosing you rather than some other competent interior designer, however, because you have studied psychology as well as design. They feel you are thus doubly suited to their particular needs.

The neurologists treat patients with a variety of chronic and acute conditions such as epilepsy, Tourette's Syndrome, Alzheimer's disease, and multiple sclerosis. Some of their patients have suffered head trauma as a result of accidents. Some are wheelchair-ridden. For many, coming to see the doctor is itself traumatic, difficult, and embarrassing. Therefore, both the physical and psychological needs of patients require consideration.

The accompanying plan shows the space they are moving into (see Figure on page 18). The doctors will be leasing only 2,600 square feet of the space; the rest will be rented to another tenant. It is an open, rectangular area with windows on two walls and some interior structural columns. (When you plan, try to bury the columns in walls.) There are main entry doors, but they can be moved if necessary; you can locate the emergency exit any place along the wall that abuts the hallway, but preferably as far as possible from the main entrance.

The doctors have the following functional requirements:

1. *Reception area:* Here, they need three 8′ × 8′ workstations for secretary/receptionists; each secretary serves one doctor. They need seating for twelve to fifteen people and a coat closet for visitors.

2. *Three doctor's offices:* Each should be about 9′ × 12′ and should be located on a window wall. Doctors' offices must be wheelchair-accessible.

3. *Three exam rooms:* Two should be about 8′ × 10′, but the third must be about 10′ × 12′. All require 5′ of lower and upper cabinets with a sink, an exam table 20″ wide × 59″ long, a visitor's chair, and a doctor's chair. The large exam room will also contain testing equipment that you do not have to show on your plan. The

exam rooms should be located near the doctor's offices (see below) and may be interior spaces. Exam rooms must be wheelchair-accessible. The large exam room must be able to admit a stretcher.

4. *A wheelchair-accessible bathroom:* The accompanying illustrations (see page 81) shows requirements for barrier-free design.

5. *A nurse's station:* This may be a small space, the size of the bathroom, with a sink and counter for a sterilizer. This is where the nurse draws blood. It can be designed as an alcove rather than a separate room.

6. *An office* 9′ × 12′ for the office manager, with a window.

7. *A computer room* near or next to the office manager, with three workstations and room for a small computer, which is about 2′ × 2′. This room may be interior space if necessary.

8. *A file and equipment room* near the office manager and also easily accessible to the secretaries. This room will contain the fax machine, the copy machine, and about twenty vertical file cabinets (15″ wide × 30″ deep). Items # 6, 7, and 8 should be clustered, if possible.

9. *A kitchen/conference room:* This room serves a dual purpose. It

must contain a full-size refrigerator, about 6' of upper and lower cabinets, a sink, and countertop space for a microwave. It should also contain as many storage cabinets as possible for medical and office supplies. In addition, the doctors need a table with seating for six to be used as either a lunch table or conference table.

10. *A "doctors' station":* This is an area of "cubbies" or wall-mounted storage bins for mail, messages, etc. It should be located centrally, accessible to the doctors and secretaries, but out of view of patients. It should be placed above a counter on which files can be rested.

11. *A closet for staff's coats.*

12. *An emergency exit:* This must open into the common area hall, must be as far as possible from the main entrance, and must be located at the end of a hallway or in a room that opens onto the interior hallway.

13. *Hallway* widths are required by code to be a minimum of 44". The doctors would like all the doors to be 36" wide to accommodate wheelchairs. Window sill height in this building is 32".

These are the factors you must consider that will have an impact on the psychological well-being of patients who come to this office.

1. *Reception area:* The secretaries often speak on the phone or to one another about matters that are highly sensitive and that they do not want patients in the waiting room to hear. Therefore, you should design their stations so that they can communicate with incoming patients and also have as much privacy as possible. Patients also may wish some degree of privacy while they are waiting. This is a difficult requirement to satisfy, but if you can, lay out the waiting room with seats organized in clusters separated slightly from one another, rather than in one or two long rows. Seating should be comfortable, since the waits are sometimes long.

2. *Doctors' offices and exam rooms:* These should be planned in such a way that each doctor has her exam room adjacent to her office. Doctors' offices should be furnished with four visitor's chairs, in case a family conference must be held while the kitchen/conference room is in use.

3. *Kitchen/conference room:* This room will be used for both informal activities—snacks and lunch—as well as doctors' staff meetings and conferences with patients' families. Therefore, you must keep these needs in mind as you design. The finish materials will need to be appropriate to a lunchroom but must also be attractive enough for a conference room. In addition, the staff do not necessarily keep the kitchen area immaculate, and yet the doctors do not want to look at a messy food-preparation area when they bring in patients; how can you solve this problem?

4. *Finishes:* Consider durability of the materials you choose throughout the space. They should be easy to clean and long-lasting, especially in the rooms that are used by the greatest number of people, such as the waiting and exam rooms. Think about colors. If people using this space are anxious, what colors might make them feel at peace? On the other hand, patients may be depressed. What colors might cheer them up? How can you make the waiting areas pleasant spaces to be in?

PRESENTATION

Floor plan: $\frac{1}{4}'' = 1'\text{-}0''$ scale. Show layout of furniture and cabinetry within the space. Render and color to show floor materials and color selections.

Perspective or axonometric of waiting room, colored. If a perspective, show a view that best illustrates your design decisions.

27. Master Suite: A Sweet Retreat

This project—designing a luxurious master bedroom/bathroom suite—is similiar to many interior designers are hired to do, except that these clients require wheelchair accessibility, as well as attention to other issues pertaining to disability.

Joel and Barbara are moving. Joel's law firm has decided to transfer him from the West Coast to the East Coast, and he and Barbara have decided to buy a house with a large, multilevel addition. The second level of the addition is unfinished, and they want to build a luxurious master suite with a dramatic, contemporary bathroom. You have been hired to design this space (see figures on pages 80 and 82).

Joel and Barbara sold their California house at a profit, and they have given you the go-ahead to create a wonderful space, whatever the cost! They want these rooms to be a refuge from the demands of their busy lives; it should evoke an atmosphere of tranquility and elegance. The master suite is their haven from the stress and competition of their workdays.

This space is particularly important to them since Barbara has become confined to a wheelchair. Diagnosed ten years ago with multiple sclerosis, her disease has recently taken a turn for the worse, and she can no longer walk. Using her wheelchair, however, she is still working full time, shopping, and trying to maintain a normal life. Therefore, although she needs barrier-free space, she does not want to sacrifice beauty or luxury.

You are given the accompanying plan and section. Your clients' functional requirements for the bedroom are: a king-size bed, two comfortable chairs with a small table, and as much closet space as possible—as much as 10' per person would not be too much. In the bathroom they would like: a double vanity or long counter with two sinks spaced well apart, lots of drawer and linen closet storage, a whirlpool tub (minimum dimensions 6' × 3'), a stall shower (minimum 3' × 3'), and a toilet. The latter should be separated partially or fully from the rest of the bathroom; it could be in a little room with a door or simply have a wall built next to it to give a sense of privacy.

In laying out this master suite, think about the flow of space.

Walls do not have to be straight; perhaps curving or zig-zag walls would create a sense of drama. The space overlooks conservation land, so the couple would like both bedroom and bathroom to share the view.

You must also consider, of course, wheelchair accessibility throughout the space. The accompanying illustrations (see page 81) give you information about barrier-free design. In addition, consider other ways in which selections of finishes and layout of furniture can be safety hazards. Floor materials can be slippery; low, small, easily overturned pieces of furniture may be dangerous; sharp edges of furniture, as well as small rugs and mats, may present a hazard to a disabled person; the use of mirrors and glass enabling Barbara to see around corners should be specified in your plan in locations where collisions might occur; level changes are inappropriate to someone in a wheelchair; good lighting will be especially important.

Once you have laid out the space, Joel and Barbara would also like suggestions from you on finishes and fixtures for the bathroom and bedroom. Visit showrooms and re-

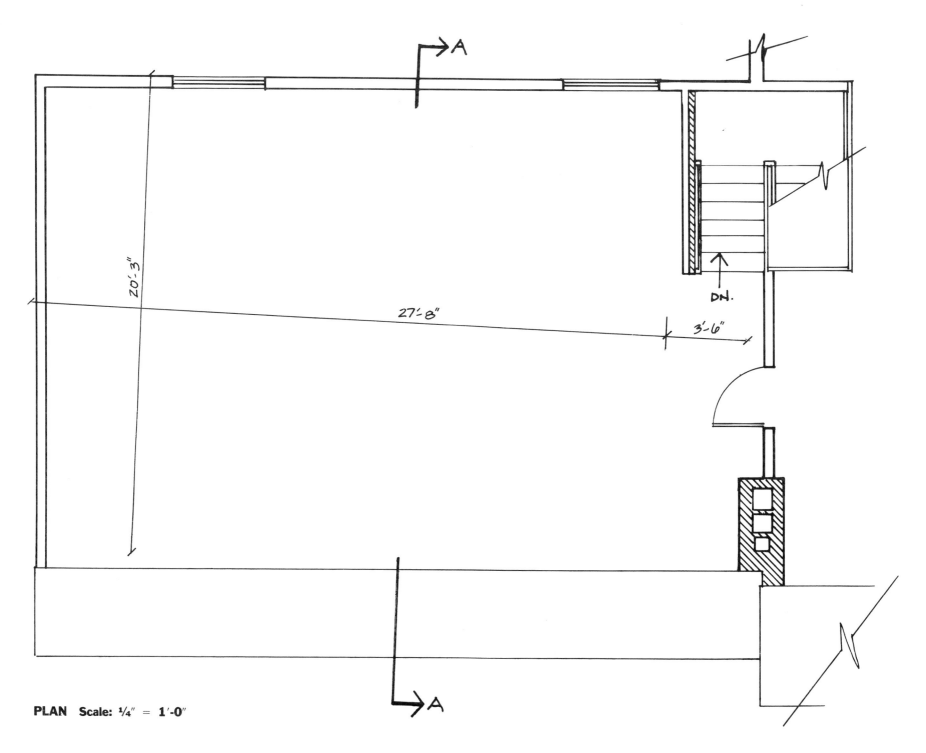

A

20'-3"

27'-8"

3'-6"

DN.

A

PLAN Scale: ¼" = 1'-0"

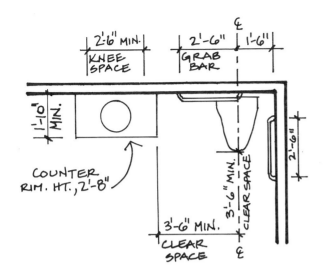

2'-6" MIN.
KNEE SPACE

2'-6" GRAB BAR

1'-6"

1'-10" MIN.

COUNTER RIM. HT., 2'-8"

3'-6" MIN. CLEAR SPACE

3'-6" MIN. CLEAR SPACE

2'-6"

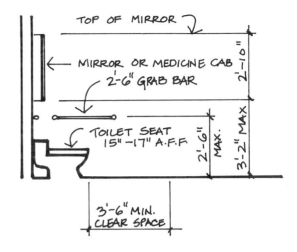

TOP OF MIRROR

MIRROR OR MEDICINE CAB

2'-6" GRAB BAR

TOILET SEAT 15"-17" A.F.F.

2'-0"

2'-6" MAX.

3'-2" MAX

3'-6" MIN. CLEAR SPACE

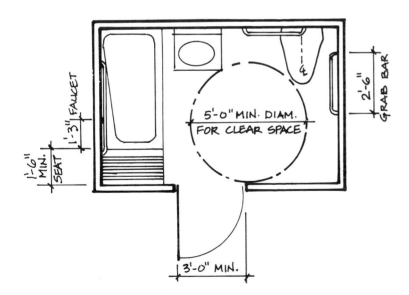

GRAB BAR

2'-6"

5'-0" MIN. DIAM. FOR CLEAR SPACE

1'-3" FAUCET

1'-6" MIN. SEAT

3'-0" MIN.

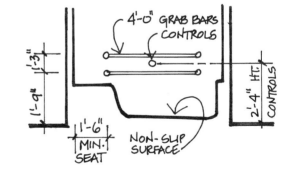

4'-0" GRAB BARS CONTROLS

1'-3"

1'-9"

1'-6" MIN. SEAT

NON-SLIP SURFACE

2'-4" HT. CONTROLS

PLANNING FOR BARRIER-FREE BATHROOMS

tailers near you to find out what products are currently available and to get information on types of fixtures and materials. Study magazines for ideas on the latest in bathroom design. Modify your choices as necessary to satisfy the specialized needs of these clients, as suggested above.

The following list will guide you in making final selections for the bathroom:

1. *Lighting:* Natural, by means of windows and/or skylights, incandescent, or fluorescent.

2. *Fixture materials:* Enameled cast iron, enameled steel, stainless steel, vitreous china, or fiberglass.

3. *Fixture styles:* Note that there are new and interesting products that have been designed to meet the needs of disabled persons.

4. *Flooring materials:* Ceramic tile, marble, granite, or other stone tile, vinyl tile or sheet, carpet, wood.

5. *Wall materials:* Wallpaper, vinyl wallcoverings, wood, marble tile, plastic laminate, vinyl sheet, wood paneling.

6. *Countertop material:* Ceramic tile, plastic laminate, marble, or other stone, Corian, etc.

7. *Ceiling material:* Gypsum board, wood, acoustical tile.

8. *Color and pattern:* Possibilities are endless!

PRESENTATION

You need to wow Joel and Barbara with your design; they are fussy clients. Make your drawings beautiful and mount them on boards.

Floor plan: ½″ = 1′-0″ scale, showing entire master suite with furniture, fixtures, and materials, rendered in color.

Axonometric or perspective(s) of the bathroom, rendered.

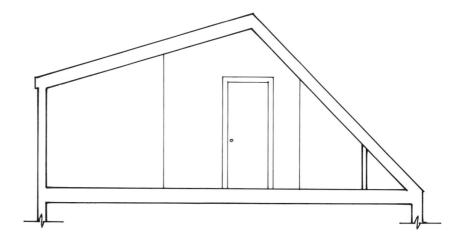

SECTION A-A

Scale: ¼″ = 1′-0″

Last year, Kim's mother, Gina, suffered a stroke, and although she is not entirely incapacitated, she has difficulty caring for herself. As a result, she is now living in a nursing home not far from Kim, who visits often.

The accompanying plan and elevation show the patient room Gina shares with another resident. It is a fairly common layout. When Kim visits, however, Gina expresses her dissatisfaction with the room, complaints which many of the nursing home residents would echo.

The principal problem here is lack of privacy, especially acoustical. Visual privacy can be achieved by pulling hospital-type draperies around the bed, but if a private conversation must be held, there is no way to prevent the roommate from overhearing it.

Gina's other complaints include the fact that there is insufficient closet space and only one dresser, which the roommates must share. Kim has discovered, to her surprise, that there is only one chair for visitors, so that if Gina's roommate has company, or if Kim brings her husband with her, some

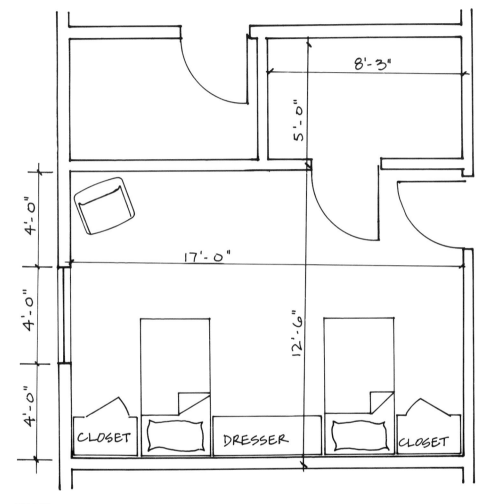

PLAN

Scale: ¼″ = **1′-0″**

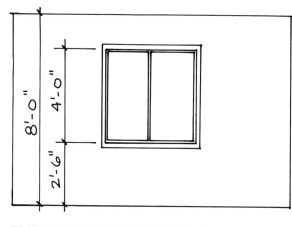

ELEVATION OF WINDOW WALL

Scale: ¼″ = 1′-0″

visitors have to sit on the bed. Gina and her roommate also share a TV and radio, which can create friction. (However, two televisions used simultaeously would not be feasible.) In addition, the positioning of the beds also means that whoever is farthest from the bathroom will disturb the other in going to use it at night.

Finally, with this layout, only one patient really benefits from the window. In this case, Gina's roommate is near the window; all day, she sits up in bed staring out. Gina's bed is too far from the window to give her a view or to allow her to enjoy a breeze if the window is open.

Both Kim and Gina feel the colors, furniture, and paintings are too in-stitutional in character; their neutrality and predictablity are depressing. They wish that patients could have a voice in the decoration of the rooms. At the very least, more interesting fabrics and carpets could be provided, and the patients could be permitted to decorate their own spaces.

How would you address Kim's and Gina's concerns? What changes in layout and decoration could be made to increase patient comfort? How would you deal with the problem of lack of acoustical privacy? Keep in mind that when you select furniture and finishes, you must consider issues of safety for the disabled and elderly. For example, furniture with sharp edges, small rugs, mats, and poor lighting can all present hazards.

Using the figures on page 81 as a guide, design the bathroom. Provide wheelchair-accessible fixtures, doors that swing out (in case an injured person is lying on the floor, preventing its inward swing), grab bars near the toilet and tub or shower. The current recommendations concerning bathroom fixtures for the elderly are that showers are safer than bathtubs, which cause more falls, and that standard toilets, with grab bars nearby, are the best choice in terms of comfort and safety.

PRESENTATION

Floor plan: ¼″ = 1′-0″ scale, with furniture, materials, and color selections shown.

Perspective, rendered in color, showing the room as it would look if occupied by two people.

Kim's mother was moved a year ago into a nursing home, after she had a stroke that left her unable to care for herself. Kim has visited her mother frequently during this time and has become very familiar with the home and its residents.

The accompanying plan and elevations show the layout of the main corridor, the nurse's station, the elevators, and the lounge. The lounge is furnished with round tables and chairs, where residents may play cards or games and with sofas grouped around a television set. It is a big, comfortable room with lots of windows to admit light and provides a pleasant view. Nevertheless, Kim has noticed that it is virtually empty all the time. Although the residents are supposed to gather in the lounge to socialize—this was the intent of the nursing home director and the architect/designer—they actually prefer to congregate in the hallway around the elevator and the nurse's station, where "the action" is! The residents pull chairs out of the lounge into the hallway or use chairs intended for visitors, which are already there, and sit for the entire day. Kim has noticed that, at any particular time, four or five people at most might use the lounge, while the rest are lining the halls. Thus, the existing layout, a typical one for nursing homes, is not serving their needs.

Kim has also noted that when she comes to visit her mother, they do not have a private place to meet. Whether they are in her mother's room and her roommate is present or they are in the big lounge, they do not feel they can speak unreservedly. In this respect, too, the existing design is not meeting the residents' needs. It seems that this design more closely reflects ideas the designers and planners hold about the elderly than it does the reality of their lifestyle.

If the nursing home director called you in to make some changes, how would you alter the plan to accommodate the residents' desire to sit and watch the activity that surrounds the nurse's station, as well as to provide space for TV watching, card games, and private "conference" areas? The director has agreed that you may make changes to the layout of interior partitions, as long as you do not enlarge the building. What recommendations would you make concerning the design and furnishings of the lounge?

In addition, since the residents spend so much time sitting in or looking at the hallway, how would you design the hall so that it is not monotonous? Can you make it residential in character and scale, through changes in ceiling heights, recessed doorways, and changes in color and texture? Your corridors must be at least 8' wide and should be provided with handrails at a height of 36". (Keep in mind that the lounge area is to be used for quiet conversation and television viewing, as described above, and is not an activity room. Elsewhere in the nursing home, there are large rooms used for performances, craft activities, etc., but that is not your concern here.)

PRESENTATION

Floor plan: $\frac{1}{4}'' = 1'\text{-}0''$ scale, showing existing, demolished, and new partitions (see bottom right illustration on page 102), with furniture layout, and rendered in color.

Perspective drawing of an important part of your design, showing your suggestions for furnishings, finishes, and lighting.

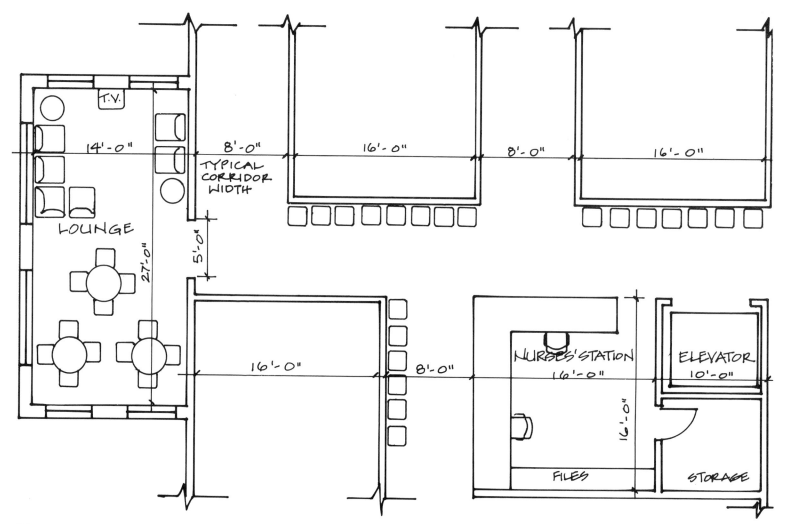

14'-0" **8'-0"** **16'-0"** **8'-0"** **16'-0"**

T.V.

TYPICAL
CORRIDOR
WIDTH

5'-0"

LOUNGE

27'-0"

16'-0" **8'-0"** NURSES' STATION ELEVATOR

16'-0" **10'-0"**

16'-0"

FILES STORAGE

PLAN

Scale: ⅛″ = **1′-0″**

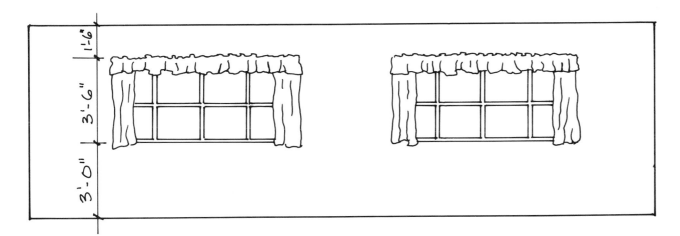

ELEVATION OF WINDOW WALL IN LOUNGE

Scale: ¼″ = **1′-0″**

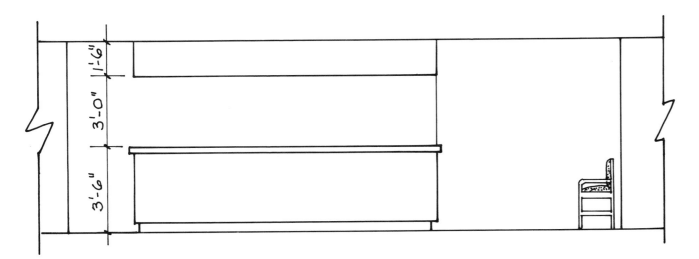

ELEVATION OF NURSE'S STATION

Scale: ¼″ = **1′-0″**

30. Your Classroom: Redesigning Is Redefining

Suggested materials: carpenter's ruler, tape measure or yardstick, roll of tracing paper, lead holder, lead and lead pointer, architect's scale, triangles, T-square, and templates (optional).

Whoever you are, and whatever your school, you are probably sitting in a big room filled with drafting tables. There are probably also a blackboard and bulletin board, and there may be cabinets, pegboard, or other facilities for storage of materials samples. You may be in a room with windows and a view or in an interior space (perhaps with skylights). The space may be new or old. The likelihood is that your tables are lined up in rows facing the front (where your teacher stands or sits at a desk).

Usually, classrooms are set up this way without forethought or analysis. Sometimes, however, the teaching method or the students' particular task will require a different layout. In Montessori elementary schools, for example, where students work on independent projects in ungraded classrooms, desks are set up back to back in clusters of three or four, and large, carpeted areas are left open for stu-

dents to spread materials out and work on the floor. This kind of classroom layout ensures that some students can find places to work alone, while others work together on projects. Many different activities can take place simultaneously in the Montessori classroom. In New York City some public school classrooms are now being built in a Z-shaped configuration rather than in the traditional, rectangular shape. The change in classroom shape permits the teacher to supervise students seated in formal rows while also monitoring the activities of students doing independent study in alcoves at the sides of the space. Although different from the Montessori model, this new design also permits a variety of learning activities to take place, while it emphasizes the traditional relationship between teacher and students. Large training and demonstration rooms in corporations running training sessions sometimes have desks or tables laid out in a big U or large circle. This kind of configuration encourages participants to look at and communicate with one another. The point is, there are many ways to plan a classroom, and the layout will affect the way in which the teacher and students

interact and the way in which learning takes place.

In the following exercise you will be asked to think about the organization of your own classroom and about the way in which the layout affects the way in which your teacher teaches and you, the students, learn. The purpose of this problem is, in large part, to encourage you to think about the way you, your classmates, and your teacher interact and about the relationship between that interaction and the design of the room.

To prepare for this project, measure your room and its components (both movable and built-in). Make a list of all items. Draw a plan to $\frac{1}{4}'' = 1'\text{-}0''$ scale, showing the room and its built-ins only.

Next, using inexpensive trace and working quickly, make drawings showing as many variations as possible on the layout of your tables. Try setting them up in linear fashion, in clusters of various kinds, on the diagonal, and in any other ways that come to mind. Think, too, about the organization and placement of materials samples if they are also located in this room. Are they readily accessible? Well organized? They may be placed at the back; should they be relocated to the sides, the front, or the center of the room? On the other hand, perhaps they should be located in another room, so that the activity of students examining and talking about materials does not distract those who are at their tables. Consider lighting; is it adequate?

In sketching the different layouts, you must consider the way in which these layouts affect your methods of thinking and working. Sometimes, students prefer to work at home and find it difficult to get work done at school; other students like to work in the company of classmates and find the presence of others helpful and inspiring (rather than distracting). It may be that the best solution to the organization of your room is a combination of tables placed apart from the others—for those who like privacy—and tables placed together, for those who prefer working with a friend. On the other hand, it may be that at certain stages in design development you are most comfortable working alone and at other stages, you would like to interact with others.

How does the way your teacher functions affect the layout? Is he or she always standing at the front? It is likely that the teacher moves around the classroom to look at student work. How do these layouts affect circulation for both teacher and students?

How much of the teaching that takes place is in the form of lectures (with or without slides)? When the teacher speaks to the class as a group, is your distance from her a problem? Is there a table around which you can sit for group discussion?

After this, you and the rest of the class will pin up your sketches and discuss the results. You will certainly have created a large number of possible layouts. Can you agree, as a group, on the best solution? Do some "reality checking" and move your tables (and other furniture) around in some of the ways suggested by the plans. To better understand the effects of changes in layout, try leaving the desks in their new configurations for several hours while you have lecture or studio time. In the end, have you been able to improve on the original layout?

Section VII
More Design Challenges

The projects in this section do not fit neatly into the other sections of this workbook, although they require that you use the same skills and information. This group of exercises, however, introduces considerations not dealt with elsewhere.

PROJECTS

31. Neat Stuff: A Storage Unit for a Child's Room

This project requires construction drawings for a custom-designed unit.

32. A Permanent Home for a Hair Salon, Part 2: A Beautiful Exterior

You are asked to design the building's exterior, including its window display.

33. No Booth Is an Island: Design of a Trade Show Booth

The design of exhibit booths for trade shows is a specialized field which has a lot in common with retail design.

34. Student Design for Student Art

For a college of art and design, you will design a gallery/shop for the display and sale of artwork by the students.

35. Kitchen Redesign: "Plan It Again, Sam"

You will redesign a kitchen, draw up plans, elevations, and a perspective to show the client; you will then produce drawings to guide the contractor in cabinet and construction installation.

31. Neat Stuff: A Storage Unit for a Child's Room

Alex is an eight-year-old boy who loves collecting things. He has hundreds of little toy cars, plastic dinosaurs, shells, minerals, and books. He loves to draw and saves many of his pictures. Gradually, Alex's room has become cluttered with his possessions. Alex's parents would like to build a combination desk/storage unit in the area shown in the accompanying plan and section. His father is willing to build it, if he is provided with good drawings that show him how.

You have been hired to design the unit and to produce the working drawings Alex's father will need. Alex and his parents agree that the unit should be "fun"—they would like something unique, something more than just a set of shelves, cabinets, or drawers, although the unit must include these. Can you think of a way—using shapes and colors—to produce a desk/storage unit that is decorative and interesting as well as functional?

The unit must provide the following: at least 36″ of desk surface for drawing; a drawer for pencils and markers; a place for blank paper and for finished drawings; shelf, cabinet, or drawer space for his collections of cars, plastic dinosaurs, shells, and minerals; at least 72″ of shelf space for books; a place for cassette tapes; at least 36″ of shelf space for baskets that contain miscellaneous objects; a source of task lighting.

PRESENTATION
Floor plan: 1″ = 1′-0″ scale.

Elevation, rendered in color: 1″ = 1′-0″ minimum scale.

Sections as needed to show construction: 3″ = 1′-0″ scale.

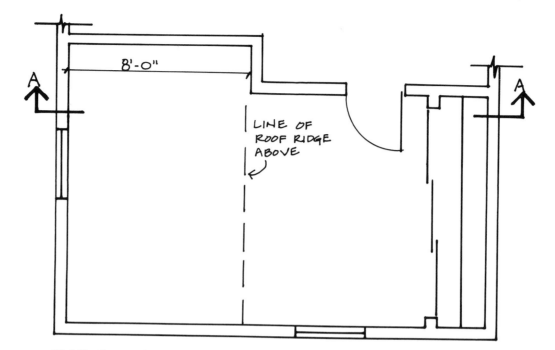

8'-0"

LINE OF
ROOF RIDGE
ABOVE

PLAN Scale: ¼″ = 1′-0″

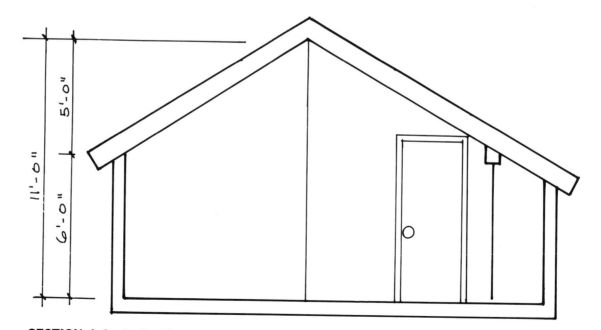

5'-0"

11'-0"

6'-0"

SECTION A-A Scale: ¼″ = 1′-0″

32. A Permanent Home for a Hair Salon, Part 2: A Beautiful Exterior

This project is a sequel to Chapter 15, "A Permanent Home for a Hair Salon, Part 1" in Section II.

If you go on to the second part of this project, you will develop the store's exterior. The accompanying exterior elevation and exterior perspective show the existing design (see exterior elevation on page 41 and Figure on page 42). The store is part of a small mall that is located on a corner in a commercially zoned district whose other storefronts are in rather uninspired, attached, one-story brick buildings with undistinguished window displays and signs.

Your design of this elevation will need to reflect the character and ambience you have created within. Above all, Jerri wants the exterior to be unique and attention-getting. You can extend the height of the building—partially or wholly —through the use of a Western-style false facade. You can use architectural details of your invention or derived from past architecture; you can use any material appropriate for use on an exterior. Jerri wants you to create unique and attention-getting signage.

In designing this elevation, you must develop window displays. Many hair salons tape big photographs of models with elaborate hairdos on their windows—this has become a cliché. What can you do instead? Perhaps you will choose to leave the windows undecorated so that the view of the interior is unobstructed.

PRESENTATION

Elevation, rendered in color: $\frac{1}{2}'' = 1'\text{-}0''$ scale minumum.

You have been asked by Wrappings, Inc., to design a trade show booth. This company manufactures and wholesales cardboard gift boxes and has made arrangements to import an attractive line of wrapping paper and ribbon made in Japan. To introduce their new lines to their buyers—card and gift shops—they have decided to buy booth space in the New York Gift Show. This is one of the largest gift shows in the country; it has thousands of exhibitors and visitors and is highly competitive.

You need to be very sensitive to the fact that the Wrappings booth will be surrounded by other booths that are bright, colorful, and appealing. The Wrappings booth must attract attention away from its neighbors. It must be beautiful, interesting, and the merchandise must be prominently displayed and well-lighted. In addition to five different sizes of boxes, Wrappings needs to display twenty-five different patterns of gift wrap, ten different solid-colored tissue papers and ten different ribbons.

The axonometric and plan give you the dimensions of the booth. Keep in mind that since this booth can

be approached from all directions, each side must be well designed and must incorporate signage. In addition to the merchandise itself, there must be somewhere inside the booth where orders can be

taken, like a table or desk. Remember that only wholesale orders are taken at the show, and no merchandise is sold directly from the booth; therefore, no storage for additional merchandise is needed.

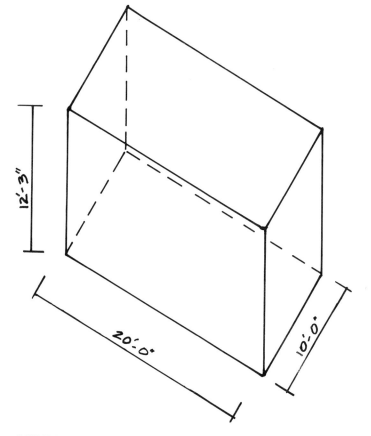

AXONOMETRIC

Scale: ⅛″ = 1′-0″

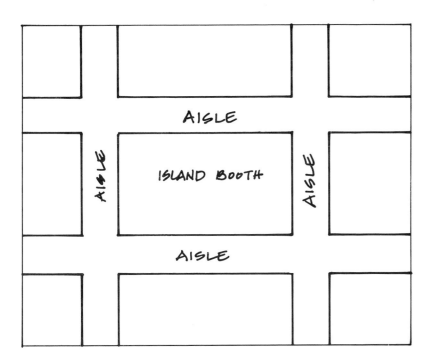

PLAN

Scale: ⅛″ = 1′-0″

The booth may be built of wood, metal or plastic; you may wish to use factory-made space-frames, lighting, or display fixtures, or you may wish to custom-design the whole booth. Any fabric may be used, but if not fire-rated, it must be treated with a chemical fire-retardant. Keep in mind that the booth will be dismantled and re-built for other shows, so all the components, including display fixtures, should be lightweight and easy to assemble.

The National Trade Show Association notes that "exhibits should not be placed on the aisle line, so visitors do not stand in and block the aisle."

PRESENTATION

Axonometric: ¼″ = 1′-0″ scale, rendered in color.

Elevation of each side: ¼″ = 1′-0″ scale, rendered in color.

34. Student Design for Student Art

The plan and elevation show a space in the basement of an older building belonging to a college of art and design. Imagine that you are a student at the college, with a major in the Department of Fashion and Interior Design. Because you are an honor student, your teacher has asked you to develop plans for this space, making it into a gallery and retail shop devoted to the display and sale of student work.

Because the work produced by students includes drawings, paintings, and small, three-dimensional artworks, as well as clothing and jewelry designed by fashion students, you will need to provide for the display of a variety of work. You should consider custom-designed display units, lighting, and the use of mannequins for clothing. It will be helpful to you to visit both galleries and retail stores to see how they deal with the display of a variety of objects. Sometimes a single object will be featured or emphasized; at other times, visual emphasis is achieved through the massing of many similar objects. As you look, think about your response to different display techniques.

Begin by making a list of all that needs to be included; do not forget storage and a sales desk, as well as signage throughout the shop. Next, make a perspective outline for the space, so that you can do some freehand sketches of displays. You should be thinking about visual merchandising issues while you are developing the floor plan. Work quickly to explore a variety of options for this space.

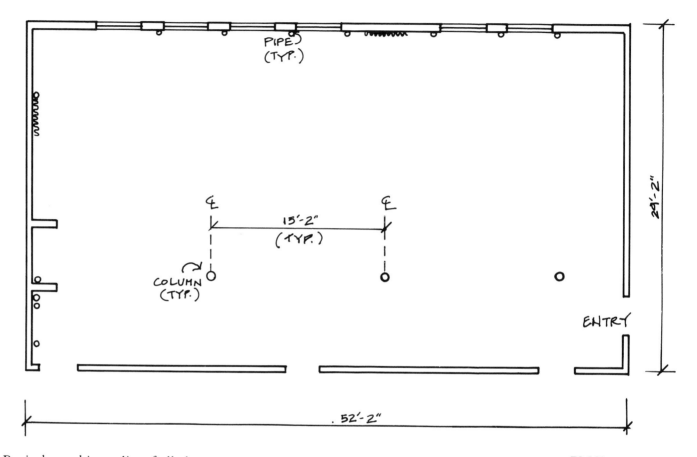

PRESENTATION

Floor plan: ¼″ = 1′-0″ scale, in color.

Elevations as needed to explain design: ¼″ = 1′-0″ scale.

Perspective: Focus on the development of a display of women's clothing.

PLAN

Scale: ⅛″ = 1′-0″

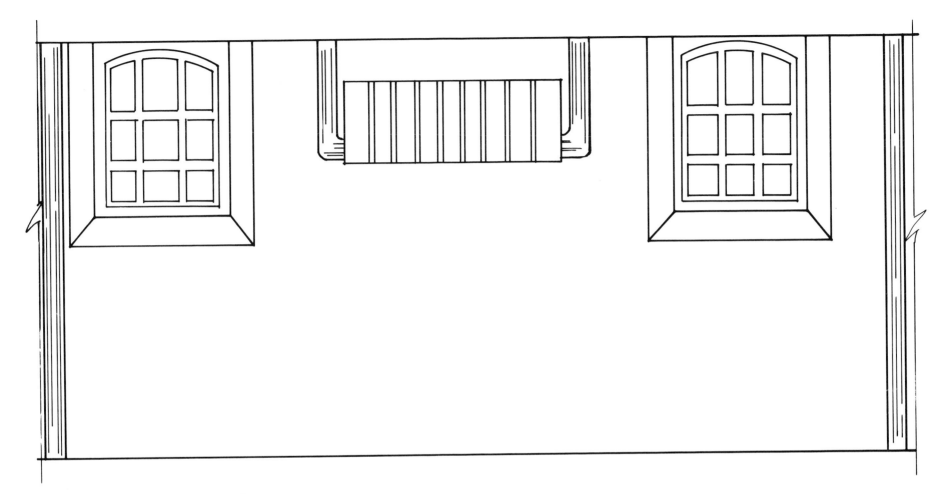

ELEVATION SHOWING WINDOWS

Scale: ½″ = 1′-0″

35. Kitchen Redesign: "Plan it Again, Sam"

The kitchen shown in the plan and section has lots of problems, some of which have to do with its relationship to other spaces in the house.

This is what the owner has to say about the existing situation.

"I hate this kitchen! First of all, when you come in my front door, you basically are entering the dining room, and you can see right into the kitchen. So when I know someone is coming, I have to rush to be sure the kitchen isn't a mess. The big peninsula doesn't make any sense, since it's dumb to have a counter with stools parked right in the dining room. Besides, it uses up so much dining room space that I can't comfortably serve more than six people. I'd like to be able to serve ten comfortably or, in a pinch, even squeeze twelve in; I'd also like the kitchen to be visually more separate from the dining room and the front door, although a pass-through would be nice.

"It would be nice to use the atrium space as an informal dining area, but right now it feels physically and visually so remote from the kitchen that it doesn't feel like they are related at all. I'd like to be able to cook in the kitchen while talking to family and friends in the atrium. So although the kitchen should be connected to both the dining room and the atrium, it should be more open to the atrium. Also, since the northern side of the house overlooks a forest, I'd like the new kitchen to have lots of windows, so I can enjoy the view.

"The floor in the kitchen and atrium has to go! I hate that tacky, flower-patterned vinyl. I'd like all the materials in the new kitchen to be light and contemporary, as well as durable, but I don't want a white kitchen; I think that's been overdone. We need to keep the cost of the renovation within reason, so instead of putting in granite countertops or marble floors or expensive Italian cabinets, we need to use medium-priced cabinets of wood or plastic laminate and tile or laminate countertops, with an interesting pattern. Appliances can be pretty standard. We need a refrigerator that's 32″ wide, a 36″-wide cooktop, a single bowl sink that's 30″ wide—I like the single bowl for washing my big pots and pans—and either wall ovens 30″ wide or a 30″-wide undercounter oven, and a place for a microwave. I'm flexible about the colors and materials, as long as I get a kitchen that's interesting and different.

"We know that the existing exterior wall will have to go, and we want to build a new wall 5′ out on the deck, so the total size of the addition will be 5′ × 13′. Of course, we expect to gut the entire existing kitchen and reorganize the whole thing."

You are provided with a floor plan and section in ¼″ = 1′-0″ scale. You need to enlarge the plan to ¼″ scale and, before beginning to sketch, to make a complete list of the client's needs. Use the layouts provided to guide you and start this project as though it were a sketch problem, by generating as many quick, alternative plans as possible within a two-hour period. You should use a scale but not your T-square or triangle, so that you are working very fast and loosely. Plan to produce one rough plan and section drawing every fifteen or twenty minutes.

When you have finally settled on an approach, you will work toward refining it. Pay particular attention to the roofline and ceiling while

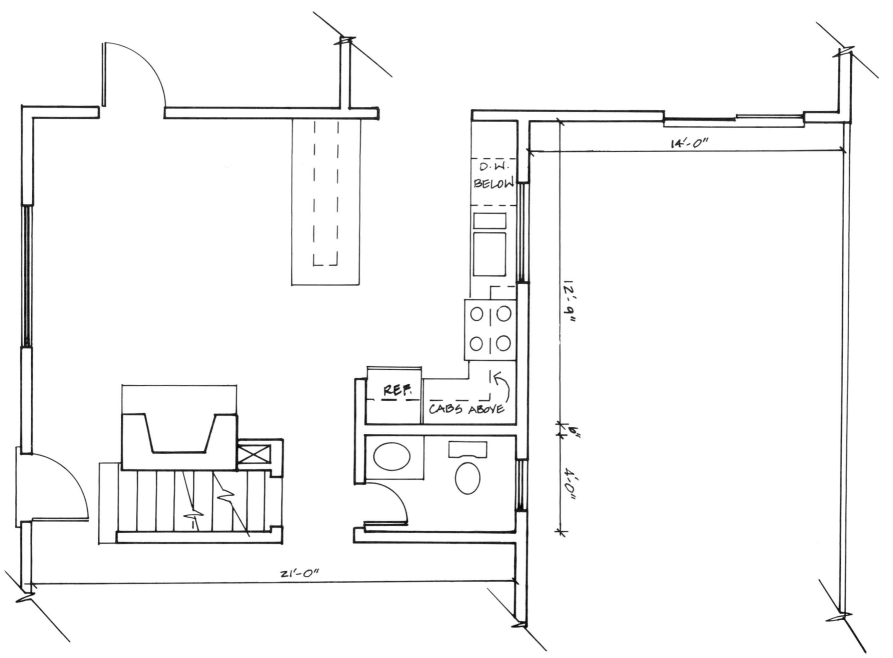

PLAN

Scale: ¼″ = 1′-0″

Text visible in plan:
D.W. BELOW
REF.
CABS ABOVE
14′-0″
12′-9″
4′-0″
21′-0″

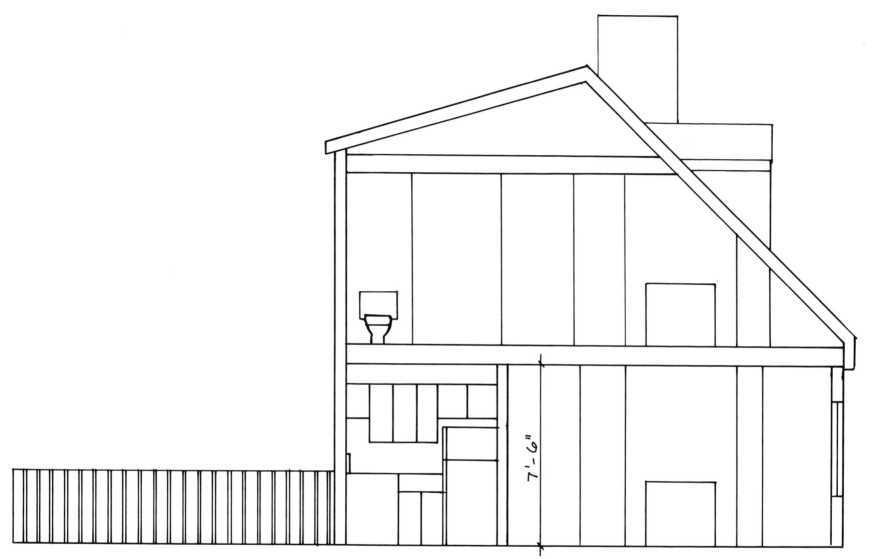

7'-6"

SECTION

Scale: ¼″ = 1′-0″

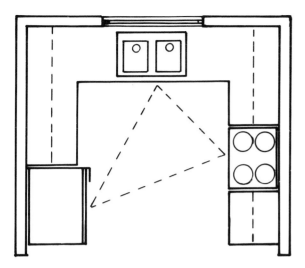

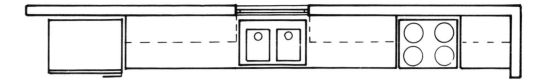

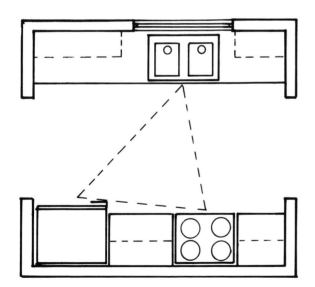

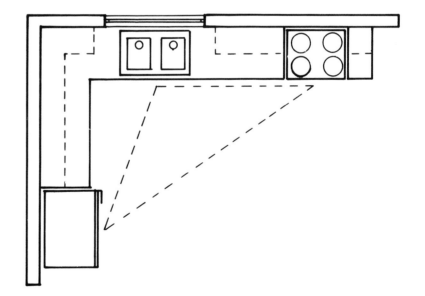

TYPICAL KITCHEN LAYOUTS

Scale: ¼″ = 1′-0″

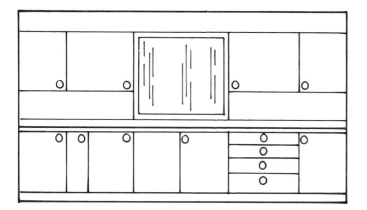

SAMPLE KITCHEN CABINET ELEVATION

Scale: ¼″ = 1′-0″

FINISH SCHEDULE

CABINETS: WOOD KING "DENMARK"
IN TEAK

COUNTERTOPS: POLISHED GRANITE
SLAB "AVERA"

FLOOR TILE A: "AVERA" POLISHED GRANITE

FLOOR TILE B: "AVERA" TEXTURED GRANITE

WALLS: EXCEL EGGSHELL FINISH LATEX
COLOR # 3563

FINISH SCHEDULE

W2430	W3630	SB48	W3630	W2430
B24	TB	B24	4DB36	B24

B: BASE CABINET

SB: SINK BASE

TB: TRAY BASE

4DB: FOUR DRAWER BASE

W: WALL CABINET

SAMPLE KEY AND SAMPLE CABINET SPECIFICATION PLAN

Scale: ¼″ = 1′-0″

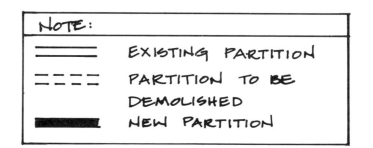

NOTE:

_____ EXISTING PARTITION

= = = = PARTITION TO BE
DEMOLISHED

▬▬▬▬ NEW PARTITION

SAMPLE NOTES

thinking about how your addition will attach to the existing house.

When you have redesigned the kitchen to your own satisfaction, you will need to produce a set of drawings that will convince your client that you have created a beautiful kitchen design in the process of meeting all of her stated requirements.

PRESENTATION

Floor plan: ¼″ = 1′-0″ scale minimum. Show cabinet and appliance layout.

Elevations: ¼″ = 1′-0″ scale minimum.

Section: ¼″ = 1′-0″ scale minimum. The section should show the relationship between the original house and the addition.

Perspective: One or two, preferably two-point. All drawings should be colored and rendered to show chosen materials.

Materials board: Finish selections may be mounted on a separate board or mounted on one of the drawings.

PART 2

You now need to produce both plans and elevations that show the cabinet selections and layout. Typ-

ically, kitchen designers produce drawings with very clear cabinets specifications and layout but that do not look exactly like architects' and interior designers' drawings. Use the accompanying illustrations that show a sample of this kind of drawing and a sample finish schedule.

In preparation for completing these drawings, you should visit a kitchen showroom and obtain a list of cabinets specifications; these tend to be relatively standard among stock cabinets. Choose a cabinet style you would like to use. With the help of the list, lay out the cabinets, taking care to consider all the details of functioning effectively in a kitchen. How will you deal with corners—by using a blind cabinet or a carousel? Where will drawers be installed? How many cabinets will be all-drawer units? How will you provide space for a microwave? Will you specify any specialized cabinets such as tall-can pantries, applicance garages, or trash drawers?

When you have completed your decision-making, draw a specifications plan similiar to that provided, with a finish schedule.

PRESENTATION

Floor plan: ¼″ = 1′-0″ scale minimum. Every cabinet and appliance must be specified.

Finish schedule.

PART 3

Another set of drawings you must provide are dimensioned floor plan and elevations. The floor plan must show the builder which walls are to be removed, which remain standing, and which ones are to be constructed. The graphic conventions for conveying this information in a working drawing are shown in the accompanying illustration. All dimensions on your plan must be shown.

Your elevations (and section/elevation, if required) should show the dimensions of all vertical elements: windows, doors, ceiling height.

PRESENTATION

Floor plan: ¼″ = 1′-0″ scale. Show existing, demolished, and new partitions in a fully dimensioned plan that indicates partitions, doors, and windows but does not include the cabinet layout.

Elevations: ¼″ = 1′-0″ scale, dimensioned.

Section VIII

Team Projects

PROJECTS

36. Everything Old Is New Again (and Again!): Renovation of an Antique House

37. What Is Interior Design? A Museum Exhibit

The projects in this section give you the opportunity to design as a member of a team. You need patience, a willingness to listen to someone else's point of view, the ability to express your own ideas, and the maturity to compromise when necessary. This is an experience that parallels that of the workplace. As a professional designer, you will work cooperatively with contractors, with your colleagues in the office, and—most important of all—with the clients for whom you design!

One of the following projects is residential and the other commercial. The latter requires that you consider the very fundamental question: What is interior design?

36. Everything Old Is New Again (and Again!): Renovation of an Antique House

Your client, Cheryl, is a financial analyst who works in downtown Boston. She has just purchased a small, 150-year-old wood frame house in Charlestown, a town directly north of Boston, and she has called you and your partners to help her lay out and decorate it. She has supplied you with plans and a section to work from.

The house is a narrow, common-wall house with a basement and three stories. Behind the kitchen is a little deck, which abuts neighboring houses and is the only "backyard" Cheryl has. The deck will remain unchanged.

This project will be done by teams of three. Each member of the team will take one floor of the house and make the redesign of that floor his or her responsibility. Thus, each member of the team will have a great deal of independence in developing a solution; however, the members of the team will need to confer with one another to be sure that the three floors of the house not only meet the client's needs but also share an aesthetic approach.

FIRST FLOOR, TO BE REDESIGNED BY TEAM MEMBER #1

Cheryl wants the kitchen replanned so that it will function better and have more storage space. Her budget is limited, so she wants to spend as little as possible on replumbing and on moving the gas line to the gas range. This does not mean that the sink or range need to stay exactly where they are, but if moved, they should be moved a relatively short distance. In fact, the range must be moved away from its location beneath the window, since both common sense and fire codes preclude leaving it where it is. The height of the windows is such that 36"-high base cabinets may be installed beneath. The brick fireplace is attractive and should not be covered up. A peninsula or kitchen table could abut the staircase. Cheryl needs her existing appliances, as shown on the plan, but wants them to be organized so that the kitchen is more functional. Currently, there is no counter space for unloading the refrigerator, there is little counter space near the stove and the dishwasher is too far from the sink. She would like storage space for food, cookbooks, appliances, pots and pans, counter space for cooking

utensils and a microwave, and either a table or counter for informal eating.

In the dining room, Cheryl would like some shelves or cabinets installed that can be used for storage. In addition, she hates the way the bathroom opens directly into the room, and she wants to eliminate the bathroom. She would like you to suggest an alternative use for that space. She needs at least a table for six to eight and a buffet, to be shown on your furniture plan.

SECOND FLOOR, TO BE REDESIGNED BY TEAM MEMBER #2

The second floor contains a guest room with an attached bathroom and the living room. Once again, Cheryl notes, there is very little storage space. In fact, the two closets shown on this floor are the only two closets in the whole house. In the bedroom she would like storage shelves or a shallow storage closet. In the living room, she wants a built-in storage unit along the window wall, with window seats; she does not want to move the radiator, so the unit must

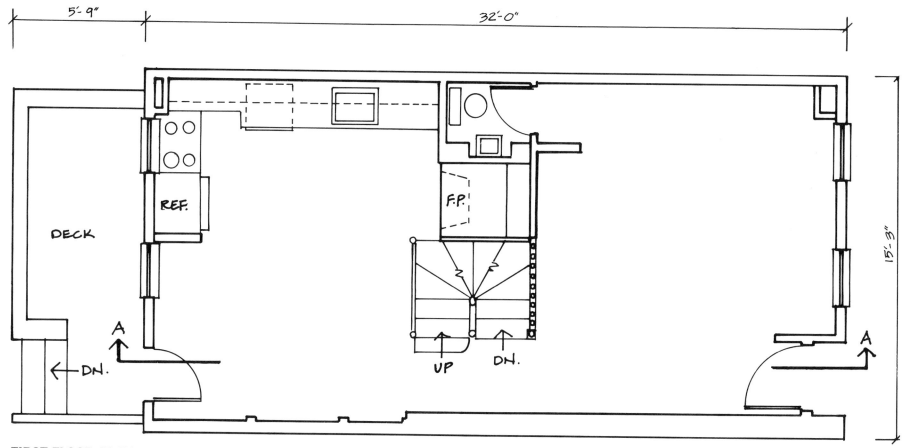

FIRST-FLOOR PLAN Scale: ¼″ = 1′-0″

5′-9″ 32′-0″ 15′-3″

DECK

REF.

F.P.

UP DN.

DN.

A

A

be designed with the radiator's presence in mind.

Cheryl wants you to do furniture plans for both rooms. The bedroom should have a double bed, dresser, and night tables. The living room should show a three-seater couch, three comfortable chairs, a coffee table and end tables. The telephone is in this room and needs a place.

THIRD FLOOR, TO BE REDESIGNED BY TEAM MEMBER #3
The third floor is unusual; it has steeply sloping ceilings that restrict headroom (see section). The bathroom was installed by an open-minded architect; it has windows in odd places and no door (see plan). This floor, which is entirely occupied by the master bedroom, has no storage space at all. Cheryl

would like you to design storage for hanging clothes, shoes, folded clothes, accessories, and so on. She would like the bathroom to be more private, but not to become cramped and closed-in or to be without light. (However, she does not plan to spend money on sky-lights.) The bedroom requires a double bed and night tables.

For all floors, you will select furniture, finishes, fabrics, area rugs to be laid on existing wide-board pine floors, and lighting. Be sure to study the plan to see what finishes there are and what should remain.

106

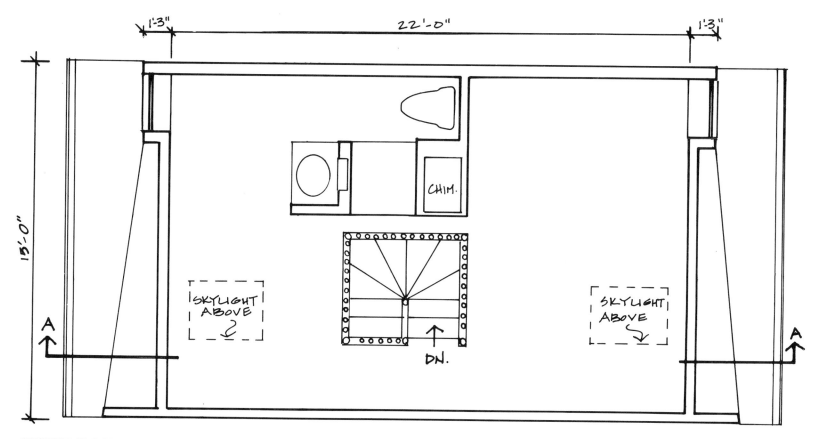

SECOND-FLOOR PLAN

Scale: ¼″ = 1'-0″

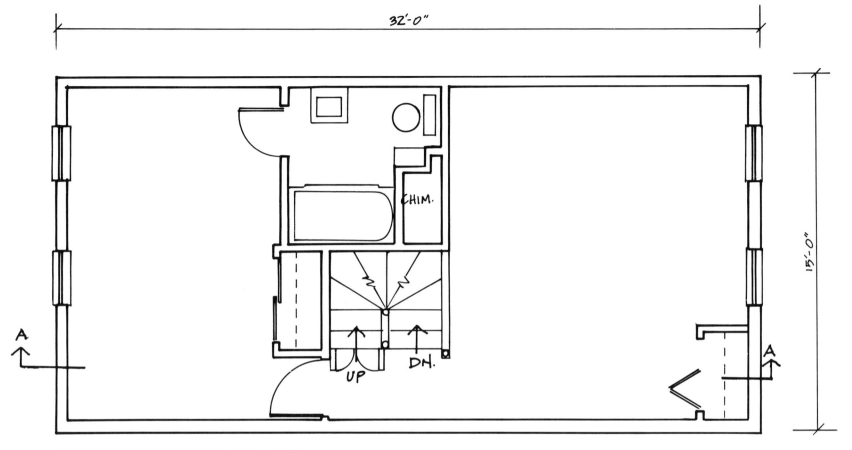

32'-0"

15'-0"

CHIM.

UP

DN.

A

A

THIRD-FLOOR PLAN Scale: ¼″ = 1′-0″

Cheryl loves Shaker-style furniture, light-colored patterned fabrics like floral chintzes and paisleys, plants, natural woods, original oil paintings and watercolors, handmade pottery, and beautiful handmade rugs. She would like this feeling of light and warmth to be reflected throughout the house, as well as in the selection of cabinets and finishes in the kitchen.

PRESENTATION

Each member of the team will produce a ¼″ = 1′-0″ scale floor plan, showing the new design, with all furniture and finishes indicated and as many notes on or adjacent to the plan as necessary to clarify the design. Elevations or sections may be required to show how new storage units have been designed; this is particularly likely to be needed in the drawings produced for the

third floor redesign. In addition, for each of the two spaces on the floor, the team member will draw a detailed perspective that reveals the furniture, pattern, color, lighting, accessory, and artwork selections. On a separate board, samples of *materials* and drawings of furniture, all clearly labeled, should be provided. All drawings should be rendered in color.

Because the entire project will be presented at once, it is important for the team members to coordinate their design approach to the presentation drawings, so that sheets are the same size and the drawings are done in the same medium. If they are mounted on boards, all the boards should be the same size and color. Title blocks must also match.

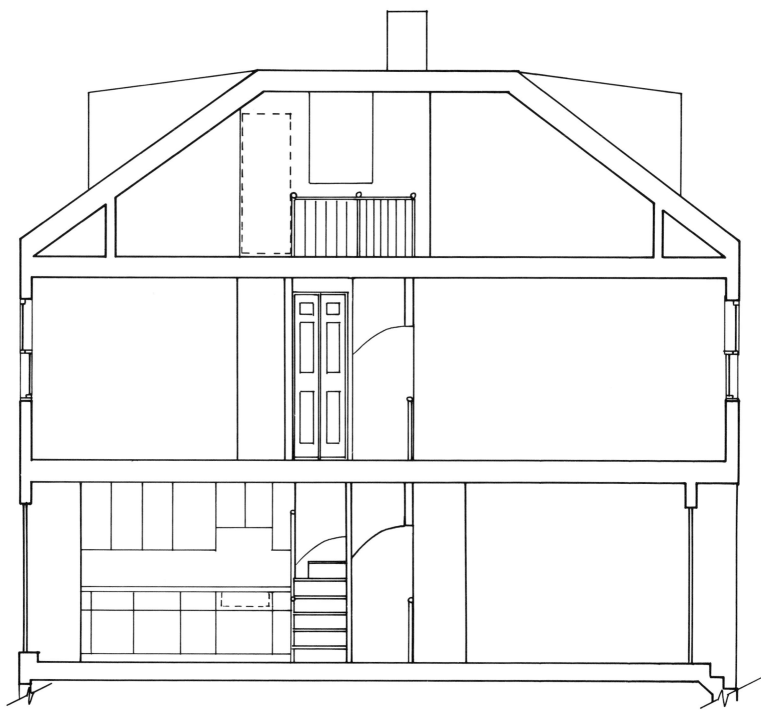

SECTION A-A **Scale:** ¼″ = 1′-0″

109

37. What Is Interior Design?: A Museum Exhibit

Choose a partner for this project with whom you think you share a point of view and philosophy of interior design. Imagine that you are the principals of a design firm that has been approached by the Education Director of a large Children's Museum. The museum plans to mount an exhibit on career possibilities. They want you and your partner to create an exhibit on interior design that explains the full scope of the field to 12- to 14-year-olds. This exhibit will be on view at the museum for several months, after which some of it will tour selected junior high schools. Because the show will be set up and taken down a number of times, it has been decided that each part of the exhibit will be presented in a demountable, $10' \times 10'$ booth, similiar to those used in trade shows.

The accompanying axonometric shows the size and configuration of the booth. It is very simple. Viewers should be able to step inside the booth and look around; you need to plan your exhibit in such a way that there is circulation space within the booth.

The first thing you do may be the most important part of designing this exhibit. The two of you must sit down and brainstorm, making a list of the basic issues and concerns with which interior designers grapple. The field is complex and varied, including as it does both residential and commercial design, and involving generalists who do it all as well as others who specialize. You need to think of *all* the problems interior designers might need to consider as they work: identifying and clarifying client needs, space-planning, the nature of materials, building codes (including handicapped accessibility), lighting, and so on. Do not forget that another part of the designer's job is to express his or her ideas in ways that are clear and persuasive. Therefore, explaining the purpose and importance of design drawings and presentation should also be a part of the exhibit. Because you obviously cannot describe everything about interior design in a $10' \times 10'$ booth, you will have to decide what aspects of the field are most important and should be highlighted here.

Your next task is to discuss the ways in which you will "teach" the viewers at the show about the topics you have chosen. Think about exhibits you have seen at places like science and children's museums. What kinds of things did you especially like and find informative? Some museums use videos and hands-on, interactive exhibits, in addition to more standard displays. You do have room in this booth for small tables which could be used to mount models or to set up hands-on displays. Take notes and make more decisions; you are refining your approach to this design. It may be helpful to talk to some young people about your ideas at this stage. Ask them what they know about interior design— it may be very little!

Next, you will proceed to sketching some of your ideas. Remembering that the design process is rarely smooth and linear, you may find that the drawings suggest further changes. You will need a very complete set of sketches, including elevations of each wall. Your job is to make the exhibit educational

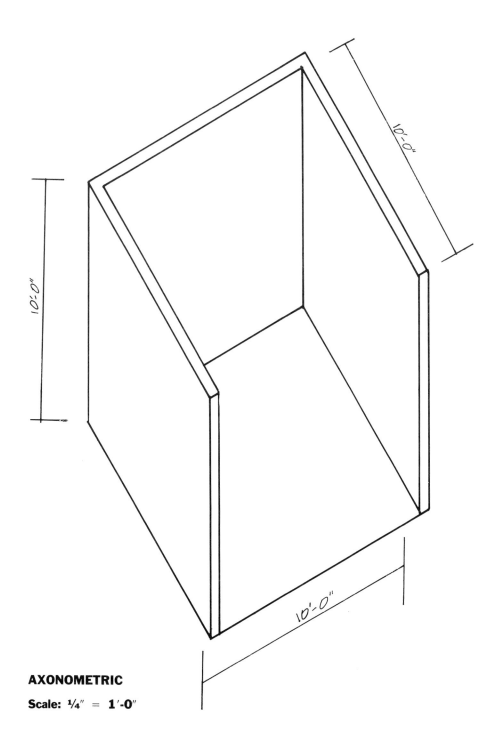

AXONOMETRIC

Scale: ¼″ = 1′-0″

and entertaining but also, of course, beautiful. Thus, as you work and sketch, think about materials and colors. (The museum will take care of ambient lighting in the space.) You can approach this part of the process by sketching together or by drawing separately and then sharing your ideas and finding ways to combine them.

Important Note: Your class may decide to approach the project somewhat differently. The following approach has the advantage that it permits the varying aspects of interior design to be explored in greater depth; it also encourages the class to work as a unit. If your class is large enough to provide at least seven or eight teams, you may decide that each team should select a *particular issue* which is explored and explained in its booth. Thus, one team may select the design process, another human factors,

another commercial finishes and materials, another codes and licensing, and so on. Get together as a group to define the issues and to decide on the distribution of the topics. Remember that you need enough topics to explain all of interior design and enough teams to cover all the topics.

PRESENTATION

Floor plan and elevations: 1″ = 1′0″ scale minimum, rendered in color. You may need notes on the drawings to explain your design.

Model: 1″ = 1′0″ minimum, of foam-core board and other materials as needed to explicate design.

Your teacher may ask you to present your work in a larger scale. You and your partner may collaborate on the drawings and model or may decide that it is better for you to divide the work.

INDEX

Note: Boldface page numbers indicate where illustrations of the indexed item can be found.